Laughing with the gods

Humor and inspiration
to help you skate through
life with a smile

Carol White Llewellyn

CommuniVision Studio, LLC

ROCHESTER, NY

Copyright © 2024 by Carol White Llewellyn

All rights reserved, except as authorized under U.S. copyright law. No part of this publication may be reproduced, in any form without written permission of the publisher.

Acknowledgement is made to BeyondtheNest.com in which various pieces of this book initially appeared.

Book and Cover Design by Carol White Llewellyn
Cover photos by Ljupco Smokovski/Shutterstock
Photos are property of C. White Llewellyn,
in the public domain, or used through
creative commons license,
courtesy of Pixaby.com or Pexels.com

Identifiers: ISBN 979-8-218-47661-8
Subjects:
Wit and Wisdom; Family and Relationships

Summary

In Laughing with the gods, author Carol White Llewellyn shares a compilation of short vignettes about the joys and challenges of being a woman, a partner, and a mother. She takes a sometimes humorous, sometimes cheeky, often poignant look at life and how to keep our wits about us and maintain a sense of humor when the world seems to be skating out of control.

First Edition 2024

To Ted, Danielle and Nicole

Forword from the Author

I credit Mr. Fields, my sixth-grade teacher, with launching my writing career. When he unveiled the box of writing prompts, I was excitedly on my way to becoming a writer. By the end of that year, I'd worked my way through  most of them. My early writing was mostly essays, poetry, and the occasional short story. It wasn't until years later, when life got more complex as I juggled career and family, that I began to write humor.

In college, I took Dr. Abraham Rothberg's Creative Writing Class at St. John Fisher College. I'd survived two previous literature courses with him, and somehow, he'd grown on me. He had a crusty Bronx accent and demeanor, a demanding, laser-sharp style of teaching, and a heart of gold that he tried hard to camouflage with a shellac of gruffness. I learned more from him than almost any other professor over the course of my academic career.

The most important work I turned in to him that year was a short story entitled, "The Diamond Cutters," based on my somewhat unsavory encounter with two unhappily-married gemologists on a train from France to Belgium during my junior year abroad in Paris.

Dr. Rothberg encouraged me to continue working on the short story, because it wasn't "finished" yet. I never completed the piece and, since this was before computers, I have no idea what happened to it. But it's still in my head and someday, I may rework and finish it. Or perhaps I'll choose, instead, to write about Dr. Rothberg, because he was a fascinating study in character. I say that with the utmost reverence.

As an inveterate writer himself, Dr. Rothberg shared vital advice, one piece of which I remember vividly.

I paraphrase him, but in essence, he declared, "You'll never feel as naked as when you write the truth. It will be like walking down 5th Avenue in New York City without clothes on."

He was right. Putting your creativity out for review is a disquieting experience. It's much like dropping your kid in the deep end and hoping those swim lessons paid off.

Most of the writing I've done throughout my career has been in a marketing capacity, for business. Around 20 years ago, I again began writing simply for the joy of it.

Shortly after my husband and I adopted our daughters, I wrote my first humor piece, "Women's Clothing, B.C. and A.D., which appeared in a now-defunct magazine with limited circulation. I didn't get paid for it, but it was exciting to see my work in a magazine for the first time. I discovered humor was a great way to amuse others while letting go of annoyance at things over which I had little control.

In 2006, I launched a travel magazine, and experienced the joy of publishing, and writing on a regular basis. Then the recession of 2008 harpooned those dreams, since one of the first things advertisers do in a recession is cut their advertising budget.

In March of 2017, Debra Ross, a dear friend I'd met during my travel magazine years, asked if I might be interested in editing a companion publication to her online parenting publication, KidsOutAndAbout.com. BeyondtheNest.com took flight, and was targeted at empty nesters. In addition to the website, customized for, and now published in over 50 cities, there is an accompanying weekly newsletter for the greater Rochester region. Each week, I write a column for it.

I am ever thankful to Deb that she entrusted me with her fledgling publication, and that she knew that I would love the opportunity to share wit, wisdom and event reviews every week. She's one of those rare individuals I truly appreciate who, when you say you'll do something, says, "Great! Here're the keys, take the car."

During the pandemic, I found it very challenging to write a weekly column because everything I wrote felt "out of sync" in a world in which people were coming down with COVID-19, and sometimes dying.

I asked our readers for their input on whether they would find humor offensive during this period, and all who responded said it would be a welcome respite. So I gingerly re-introduced humor pieces, trying to elevate the mood of a world gone dark. I also peppered the columns with inspirational and reflection pieces.

Even now, with the fragile state of our country, I sometimes wonder if humor is frivolous. Then I think of how humor and laughter connect people, and I dismiss this concern because connection is always needed, especially in challenging times.

This book is a compilation of some of my favorite pieces written over the past twenty years, but mostly in the last eight. I have chosen to organize it by genre, and then within those sections, in chronological order. Since family members and friends wander through its pages, holidays provide landmarks, and recent events, such as the pandemic, shootings and wars put their stakes in the ground, that arrangement makes the most sense. It felt as if the work would be too chaotic if it weren't arranged in some semblance of chronological order.

Although most of the pieces are personal, I tried to choose only those with universal themes.

With regard to the humor, I am an equal opportunity humorist, and never intend to offend or hurt anyone. I generally tend to shoot humor-spiked arrows at *situations*, but sometimes people just jump in front of the target!

Finally, I know how valuable everyone's time is these days, so I appreciate that you have chosen to spend some of yours with me. I hope I can pick your spirit up, make you smile, challenge you, or give you something new on which to reflect, through reading this book.

Table of Contents

Humor

Page	Title
17	Women's Clothing, B.C. and A.D.
21	Man's Oldest Survival Mechanism
25	The Wicked Witch, the Bell Jar and the Girlfriends' Getaway
29	It's a Guy Thing
31	The Season of SSAD
33	It's Only a Click Away
35	Reflections on Buffaloes and Berries
37	The Evolution of Navigation
39	How I Lost My Husband
41	Alien Testing
43	This is Your Brain on Electronic Devices
45	TV Hacking
47	Superpowers We Could Live Without
49	Time Travel: Have Your Cake and…
51	Kitchen Conspiracy
55	It's Hard to Stay Zen in Rush Hour Traffic
57	Fashion Revolution Resolution
61	Apps of Change
63	Getting to Know You
65	The Rage of Aquarius
67	Forever in Stamps
69	Taxing Humor
71	Blame It On Minute Rice
73	Animal Testing
75	Grocery Shopping by Another Name
77	Channeling Imelda Marco
79	Cooking Up a Little Trouble

Page	Title
81	Cleaning Downton Abbey
83	A lighthearted look at AI (animal intelligence)
85	In Search of the Perfect Valentine's Gift
89	Santa Pushed Me Off the Wagon
91	Confounding Google
93	A Woman's guide to (feeling like you're) losing weight
95	Of Cooties, Confessionals and Igloos
97	Where's Alice When You Need Her?
99	Symphony of Mischief
101	Who Stole My Gardening Gene?
103	Designers & Dressing Rooms, Clothing & Critics
105	Casting Around for Innovation
107	A Weighty Concern
109	A Brand by Any Other Name Would Just Smell
113	The Gnomes of Status Quo
115	Inheriting Up
117	Searching for the Bermuda Triangle
119	Clothing Revenge
121	Measuring Pandemic Clutter
123	Coming Back as a Classy Chassis
125	Communication Discombobulation
127	Kitchen Capers
129	Reclaiming Pandora's ~~Box~~ Closet
131	Déjà Vu, All Over Again
133	Collaborating with Artificial Intelligence
135	Travel Tribulations
137	Of Ovens and Athletes
139	Extreme Travel Packing
143	The Ants Go Marching...
145	Driving the Prom Queen
147	A Finite Art

Table of Contents

Poetry

Page	Title
153	Lament for Swimsuit Shoppers
155	Valentine Art
159	Prime Day Lament
161	Dieter's Dilemma
163	Sweet Memories of Winter
165	Barely Two Weeks 'Til...
167	Weight Loss Blues
169	Thanksgiving Blessing
171	Ode to Groundhog Day

Reflection & Inspiration

Page	Title
175	Au Revoir New York
179	Memories of Adoption Eve
183	Cycles of Life: Outgrowing Dolly
185	Random Acts of Kindness
187	Laughing with the Gods
189	To Live One Day Over
191	Aging Out of the Toy Aisle
193	Invisible Ties that Bind
195	Choose to Twinkle
197	In Our Mother's Steps
199	Sedona Mother
201	Father's Day Tribute
203	Reminiscence of the Dog Days of Summer
205	Symphony of the Season
207	Thanksgiving, Family & Chocolates

Page	Title
209	Finding Your Next Passion
211	What's Your Superpower?
213	Of Sand, Snowflakes, and Humans...
215	Down a Garden Path
217	Of Comets, Odds and Heavenly Bodies
219	They Can Never Be Taken Away
221	For Love of the Dog-eared Book
223	*That* Kind of Mom
227	Running Away from One Too Many.
229	Saving a Sisterhood of Starfish
231	Of Verandas, Communications and Coronavirus
233	Too Much *Feng* in Your *Shui*?
235	Preserving Mother's Day Memories
237	The Summer of the Caterpillar Coat
239	Traditions, Warm and Wonderful
241	Hoarding Memories
243	Aging Gracefully into the True You
245	Out of the Darkness: Light One Candle
247	Carpe Diem: Your Future Is In Your Hands
249	Making Time Stand Still
251	Riding a Bike at Dusk
253	Today's My Lucky Day!
255	Mother's Day Message on Live Action Parenting
259	We Are All Fireflies
261	Summer Fair Nostalgia
263	It Tastes Like Christmas
265	Excuses Masquerading as Reasons
267	Fear of the Flop
269	It's in the Cards
271	No Imposter
275	All That You Are
277	Acknowledgements

Humor

Women's Clothing, B.C. and A.D.
2005

No one can say I wasn't warned. It's not one of the things they mention in the book, *What to Expect When You're Expecting*. Its one of those nasty little secrets friends like to whisper once you're already pregnant (or in my case, once the adoption paperwork is in). By then, it's too late to turn back.

I still remember the first time I was warned. My husband and I were at a picnic for adoptive families and those waiting for referrals. We met Loreen and Stephen who were adopting their second child.

The four of us were talking about how kids change your life—*as if* my husband and I *knew*.

Loreen confided, "You know, B.C.—before children—my style was definitely *Sex in the City*. Now, A.D.—after diapers—it's more like *The Muppets Do Desperate Housewives*."

"…I'm just happy when I can get out of the house with clean clothes on," sighed Stephen.

I chuckled, thinking, "Surely, they joke."

Expectant parents are so naive. They also believe they'll never feed their kid McDonald's.

Four months after the arrival of our twin daughters, I went back to work. At the first Board Meeting following my return, I had a presentation to make in front of 30 Directors of the Board. Before leaving the house, I bent down, hugged my toddlers and said, "Wish me luck."

They did.

As I got up to take the floor, I glanced down to discover four little yogurt handprints on my thigh-length navy jacket.

Flip charts make wonderful camouflage.

Then there was the time someone complimented me on my pin.

"What pin? I don't remember putting on a pin."

There, adhered to my Fair Isle sweater, were three bright, multi-colored fruit snacks.

And I'll never forget the family photo where I have spit-up globs smeared across my left shoulder. I asked my husband, "How could you let me go out of the house looking like that?"

"Looking like what?"

Whoever invents vomit detectors for shoulder pads will make a fortune.

Now, the damage to the wardrobe doesn't stop with the food. Something happens to the clothes themselves. They self-destruct just to get even. To compound matters, they don't get replaced.

The results?

The elastic in my underwear's so stretched out that it's in testing for bungee cord. My bras are so saggy, I'm selling them on e-bay as double-barrel slingshots, and some of my shirts are so threadbare that whole quilts are begging to be fabric donors.

Worse yet, the clothes that aren't busy self-destructing are trying to turn vintage. Those blue and gray striped, flare-leg hip huggers I once wore in high school would be the rage right now if I hadn't chucked them in a donation bin a year ago. I can just see it...some teenage thrift store shopping diva has matched them with a ruffled-front flowered shirt and is parading around, the height of retro chic.

You know, I get quite annoyed when I actually *do* get out shopping. All of the clothing is designed for women under child bearing age. I've finally realized this is done with a purpose. Clothing designers are simply protecting self-interests. Gerber's on Ralph Lauren is like a Barbie sticker on a Harley.

I keep thinking that once my daughters are old enough to buy some of their clothes with babysitting money, my wardrobe will return to its former state of elegance, but I suspect I may be in for a shock. I'm haunted by the tale my friend Elaine tells about watching TV with her teenage daughter. Her daughter has been campaigning for Elaine to update her wardrobe.

"Can you believe it? She gave me a top with spaghetti straps for my birthday so I'd be 'fashionable!' I'm sorry… they're *spaghetti* straps—meant for *meatballs*, not *melons*."

She continued, "So, the other night, she and I were watching that TV show, *Your Clothes Should Be Outlawed*. You know, that reality show where they strip the worst-dressed audience members of their clothes and dress prisoners in them as a form of torture.

"Suddenly, she runs screaming from the room and comes back laughing hysterically.

'Mom, notice anything?' she asks, holding up one of my favorite tops.

"The show's fashion victim is modeling *my* sweater."

After this story, I take strange comfort in one thing: I will never have to worry that my clothes will be hijacked for college by two envious teenage daughters.

Man's Oldest Survival Mechanism
2009

Some have suggested man's oldest survival mechanism is his skill at hunting. Others have stated it's his ability to adapt. A few credit his "fight or flight" response.

I have finally figured it out. There's no doubt that man's oldest survival mechanism is his tendency to snore. Here's how I discovered it.

I'd known Rupert—Rupe for short—since we were six, which, let's just say is a long time, even in *dog* years.

When I gave up the joys of retailing and moved from Philadelphia to New York City, he and I roomed together in Astoria, Queens.

For a little over a year, Rupe and I shared an affordable little apartment, conveniently located near a rowdy neighborhood sort of corner bar, a Greek pizza parlor and a subway stop that offered mostly-quick trips into Manhattan.

Besides sharing an apartment, Rupert and I also shared opposite sides of a bedroom wall.

The one thing that puzzled me about this apartent was why, at night, the rumble and vibrations of the subway resonated so much more than in the daytime. Did the night air magnify the sound and tremors? Was there less city noise and movement to muffle it? Maybe I simply noticed it more because I was, well, *home* instead of at *work*.

I wondered about this until the first time Rupe fell asleep on the living room couch.

His snoring hit 6.8 on the Richter Scale. The downstairs neighbors asked what construction was being done in the living room. We had to re-nail seven floor boards the next morning.

Since then, I've come to realize snoring is a little-discussed survival mechanism.

You're skeptical? Just think about it.

Imagine our early ancestors: by day, a silent, stealthy and lethal predator, aggressively tracking down game for slaughter, in order to be welcomed home as the bread—make that—meat-winning hero.

But at night, the tables are turned. The predator becomes the hunted, vulnerable to the marauders of the night who would wrest him, slumbering, from his bed.

This is when snoring becomes a defensive tool. Just envision a whole encampment of hunters, exhausted from the day's hunt, groggy from the night's imbibing, sending out raucous shock waves resonating from their nasal cavities. Why, night predators must have thought the T-Rex came back from extinction.

Once safely back in the comforts of his home, man's snoring played another important role in his survival... awakening his spouse.

Now she's been home, sleeping alone, and soundly for *weeks*. Suddenly, he arrives home and with him comes his sonorous snoring threatening to bring the roof down.

She has two choices. Hit him to get him to stop. Or wake him up for a procreative romp in the hay. Which would you choose? Which would work better for the continuation of the species?

Who knew sonorous snoring was a positive attribute in natural selection and survival of the fittest?

Helping you skate through life with a smile

The Wicked Witch, the Bell Jar and the Girlfriends' Getaway

2013

Most of us love being moms. We love our families and wouldn't exchange being a mother for anything in the world. But admit it…don't you sometimes wish you could go back to *just being you* for a day? You know…the you that existed BFF (before fabulous family)? The you who splashed on perfume instead of calamine lotion, who shopped for pastel clothing two sizes smaller without concern that strained carrots or green peas might show, the you for whom a normal evening meant a cute date, a romantic dinner, a flight of wine and a night on the town, not a re-run on MeTV, a pot pie, a drink tray full of 7-Eleven Slurpees® and fanning yourself in front of a hiccupping air conditioner.

I think I was several months into motherhood before the call of the wild howled in me. I longed to throw caution to the wind and do something *really* crazy…like having private time in the bathroom or splashing on something not made by Johnson & Johnson.

But alas, guilt won out. The insidious call of deferred maternal chores beckoned. By the time I answered, I could have bungee jumped from the top of the laundry, scaled the Everest of dishes in the sink or recreated *Honey I Shrunk the Kids* in our redwood forest of grass.

I sighed, put my twin daughters down for their relay naps, fed the washing machine a seven-course dinner and made a "to do" pile out of whatever I couldn't cram into the dishwasher without dismantling it. I considered borrowing a goat for the grass, but somehow, the thought of more poop deterred me.

Then a plan hit me. It was all so simple! All I needed was a large shelf and a big bell jar. I could put my husband and daughters on the shelf, under a bell jar, where they'd be safe and sound, and time would stand still within! Then, off I would go for a weekend of restless meanderings, binge sleeping, and indulgent food remarkably free of the word "helper."

Did you know they don't sell those bell jars on the internet? Well, at least, none that said they'd stop time or fit humans.

I made it through those first few years of motherhood with only an occasional and temporary transformation that involved the word "itch" without a beginning letter of "w" or "b." Fortunately, my husband likes science fiction so he finds roaring, green-faced monsters entertaining.

Since those days, I've discovered the next best thing to a bell jar: The girlfriends' getaway. For one weekend each X weeks/months [fill in frequency depending on desperation level], you get to click your heels, wave a "wand" (that looks remarkably like a credit card) and be someplace other than home…without dropping houses on anyone.

It's amazing how a change of perspective and a little pampering can change your world from black and white back to technicolor. And before you know it, you'll be ready to click your heels again and return to those little munchkins at home!

It's a Guy Thing
2017

So, my girlfriend Elaine calls me up on February 28, perturbed.

"You won't believe it! Our cleaning lady took our Christmas tree down yesterday!"

Now, I should explain that Elaine had purposely left the tree up because my sister—who is her former college roommate—and my brother-in-law always visit them over Presidents' weekend, which is the first chance they all have to celebrate Christmas together. They do it up big, complete with gifts, dinner, Christmas music and tree clad with ornaments and lights. This year it had to be postponed a bit longer than usual.

"When I came home from work yesterday, the tree was gone, the boxes were back in the basement and our cleaning lady had put all the living room furniture back where it was before Christmas," Elaine shared in exasperation.

I thought to myself that if my imaginary cleaning lady ever did that, I'd have a fit. Then of course, I realized if I could trade in my current non-self-cleaning house for an over-zealous cleaning person, I really *could* live with that.

She added, "and you want to hear the funniest part? My dear husband came home from work before I did, changed his clothes, made dinner and never even noticed the tree was gone. You *know* he *had* to have walked through the living room *at least* four times. When I came home and shrieked when I saw the tree was down, he thought I was kidding."

"It's a guy thing," I said, thinking of the other day when....

My husband complains, "Carol, we're out of popcorn."

"I *just* got back from the grocery store! Why wasn't it on the shopping list?" I ask, somewhat miffed.

"What shopping list? I keep hearing about this mythological shopping list that lives on the refrigerator, but I never see it!"

"It's here," I say, pointing at the bright red and green hard-to-miss holiday-themed 3" by 8" shopping list stuck magnetically to the front of the fridge, complete with corresponding pen.

"Well, I never noticed it before. The refrigerator's big."

Sometimes it amazes me that the human race didn't become extinct with men as the hunters.

The Season of SSAD

2017

Everyone's heard of Seasonal Affective Disorder, or SAD, that hits in the winter when it's dark and gloomy. Did you know that there's another little-known type of seasonal disorder that's equally distressing and depressing? It's called SSAD—Swimsuit Shopping Affective Disorder.

It's almost Memorial Day which means swimsuit season looms like a Dementor. I don't know about you, but I get about as excited for it as a clam awaiting a clam bake. Inevitably, I pull my prior-year suits out of my dresser and discover they have all shrunk two sizes. I don't understand how, just sitting there alone, they could shrink so much. I wish my laundry pile would learn that skill.

So it's off to the department store I go…and it darn well better happen *before* Memorial Day, or all that will be left will be thong bikinis and suits that appear to be gym bloomers, outlawed by fashionistas in the '70s.

After an hour and forty-seven minutes of rummaging through every mismatched and inside-out swimsuit on the rack, as well as those that have flung themselves to the floor in despair, I gather up the suits in my size that are even dubious contenders, and head for the dressing room.

"Excuse me Ma'am. You can take three in with you. Just leave the rest on this rack. You can come back out and exchange them," instructs a size negative-three sales minion.

What?!! Does she not know what it takes to disrobe, shimmy into each rubber-glove-swimsuit, then re-robe this voluptuousness to make the exchange, not once, not twice, but thrice-and-a-third times?

As I step with my three suits, into the room I've apparently been assigned (since a word that looks more like "Caraway" than my name is scribbled on the door's chalkboard), I realize this store did not get the fitting room memo.

Joan Lincoln, Tony Infantino's *Fashion First* Consultant on the WARM 101.3 morning radio show, advises retailers to use peach-colored lighting in dressing rooms. Soft white lights with a gentle peach tint give a "most pleasing and flattering effect." Pleasing and flattering is not what awaits me in my dressing room mirror. I look a lot like Mrs. Shrek in a fun house mirror on a bad bathing suit day, thanks to the gracious green glow of the lighting.

On my third trip to get three of the four remaining suits, I discover they are all missing from the rack.

"Oh, were those yours?" Miss size negative-three asks in a bemused tone that hints only remotely at apologetic. "I'm so sorry. I put them back."

With a sigh, I decide fate has spoken.

As I leave the store without trying on my final four choices, I realize I just *might* appreciate a return to bloomers.

It's Only a Click Away
2017

For the life of me, I can't figure out how hackers can get into my online accounts, when I can't.

You've probably had that experience of trying to place an order, typing in your surefire password, and getting one of those flippant little messages: "The password you're trying to use belongs to your dog. Please try again."

Well, it's possible you made a typo—when all the letters appear as ******, it's easy to make a mistake. If they're going to camouflage the pin, the least they could do is use dollar signs.

With your next attempt, the message reads: "You just don't give up, do you? Try again."

They might as well say, "Go to jail. Go directly to jail. Do not pass Go. Do not collect the goods in your shopping cart."

After one more insult-ridden attempt, you beg for your password to be sent to your email. You open the email. At last...the magic key to the magic door of the wonderful magic shopping cart!

Instead of your password, "Click to reset password" appears.

"But that's not what I want!" you shriek at the computer along with a few choice words, as if expletives work the same as "Open Sesame" in Ali Baba and the Forty Thieves.

You try your old password twice more. The final attempt reveals the real reason you can't get in: "Password expired. CPR will not resuscitate."

Resigned, you give in and reset the password to something you hope you'll remember, but "just in case," you add it to your spreadsheet of 373 other passwords.

Then, as if it's a Magic 8-ball, a message slowly appears: "Password invalid. Password must contain two rhyming words, three consecutive syllables, five numbers that add up to seven, your blood type, and a partridge in a pear tree."

At last, you find a password that passes muster. You click "submit," and a box appears next to the message: "To confirm your password, do three laps around the house, shine your kitchen windows for Pete's sake, and enter the 74 digit code we just sent you to an email you probably no longer use."

Finally, short on breath and having jumped every hurdle, you access your shopping cart, delighted to finally have the satisfaction of clicking "submit order."

Across your screen appears the message every online shopper dreads: "Time expired. Please start over."

Who knew shopping carts were mind-controlled by stingy spouses?

Reflections on Buffaloes and Berries
2017

The other night my husband shouted from the kitchen, "Hon, where's the tartar sauce?"

"In the door of the fridge, top shelf."

"I looked. It's not there."

"It was when I was making dinner."

"Not there. I checked."

"Trust me. It's there."

I hear the refrigerator door open a third time.

"Nope, not there."

I sigh, go to the fridge, open the refrigerator door and pull the tartar sauce from its place of honor… on the right side of the refrigerator door, top shelf.

"The label's different," he mumbles as I hand it to him.

I can hear many of you women nodding your heads in agreement. I bet there are very few women who *haven't* had this experience. It goes along with the chapters on "Why Real Men Don't Ask for Directions," "Why Real Men Don't Use Calendars," and "Why Real Men Don't Tell You Your Hair Looks Like It's Been in a Cotton Candy Machine."

I finally realized that it all comes down to evolution. You know…buffaloes and berries.

You see, waaay back at the dawn of humanity, men were hunters of very big, roving things (Buffaloes), and women were gatherers of very small, stationery things (Berries).

Basically, that explains it all (including differences in communication styles).

Don't believe me? Well, think about a group of hunters out on the plains, stalking a herd of wild buffalo that will provide food and clothing for their clan for weeks to come. They follow the herd for miles upon miles, days upon days. They identify their target and fan out, waiting for just the right moment to strike.

Now imagine the guy who turns to his fellow hunters and shouts, "Hey, guys, what direction do you think they'll move next?"

He'd, no doubt, fall victim to the slings and arrows of outrageous misfortune.

If you find it hard to understand why your guy can't seem to find household items that seem to be staring him in the face, it helps to understand that the fine-tuned, small-object "search and secure application" has become a recessive trait, bred out of Male 6.0. It also explains why guys will notice any high-end sports car anywhere on the road, no matter how far away, but won't notice when you're missing one of the earrings you had on when you left the house.

Yup. Good thing those buffaloes never figured out how to disguise themselves behind berry bushes.

The Evolution of Navigation
2017

I have a reputation for being directionally challenged. I blame it on evolution. Men clearly have an edge in the navigation department. If my female ancestors had been hunting buffaloes (at long distances) rather than gathering berries (nearby), I bet I'd have a better sense of direction today.

In theory, you're not lost as long as you have an accurate map and a full tank of gas. In reality, you can waste a lot of time and gas being "not lost."

So, I've learned the hard way to never go anywhere without my GPS. Also, a map, in case of spontaneous GPS combustion or defection.

My initial GPS was named Lee. Lee had a lovely "Outback" Australian accent. When I first got him, he had a full head of (I'm imagining blonde) hair. By the time Lee "retired," he was bald from pulling it out. "Recalculating" was his favorite word.

I now own a GPS named Barbara. She has a soft, sultry voice and doesn't even curse when I detour. I have to say, though, she has taken me on some seriously wild goose chases. I can't figure out whether she suffers from ODDD

(Occasional Directional Deficit Disorder), or she takes an occasional nip to deal with my whimsical direction following.

Honestly, I don't know what I'd do without my GPS… although I must admit I haven't seen nearly as much of the country as I did when maps were my sole guide.

For example, I'm one of only two individuals (both of whom happened to have been in the same car) who can claim the distinction of driving from Rochester, NY to the Pocono Mountains (in eastern Pennsylvania) by way of Erie, Pennsylvania (as far west in the state as you can go).

In my defense, it was night, and we had no GPS. But when I passed a large, well-lit casino that had never been on that route during daylight hours, you'd think I'd have gotten suspicious. We spent an additional 4.5+ hours and 257 miles being "not lost" on that trip from Rochester to the Poconos.

While I do like my GPS, I'm really waiting for the self-driving car. According to an article on autonomous vehicles, there are five levels of automation in self-driving cars, with one being the lowest and with four being, well, "a car you could sleep in."

If the level five car guarantees you can't get lost, I'll be first in line to buy one.

Once I find the dealership.

Helping you skate through life with a smile

How I Lost My Husband
2017

I must admit, it was probably my own fault, but I really didn't see it coming. It was Christmas day four years ago when I first introduced them. I should have realized the way my husband looked at her spelled trouble. It happened slowly, little by little at first, so I barely noticed the difference. Initially, he was his same attentive self, but slowly I noticed his attention wandering more and more.

Before she appeared, we did things together—sometimes dancing or plays, movies or art exhibits, dinner out…. Soon though, she seemed to have him mesmerized.

The thing is, I wouldn't have suspected how spellbound he would become, because she really wasn't his type… flat in front, but broad, and not really that much to look at, until…. Then, there was no contest.

As far as I could tell, she couldn't actually *do* much. Oh she could *talk* a fine tune about cooking, and she could share all the best recipes by all the most reputable chefs, but you wouldn't catch her near a frying pan or stove. And she was a wealth of knowledge on fashion, home décor and remodeling, real estate, and any other number of subjects, but heaven forbid she should actually make a move.

The thing is, I just couldn't compete with her ability to talk about almost any topic….politics or science, finances or even weather patterns. When she went on and on about news or science fiction, he could barely take his eyes off her. How's any woman supposed to compete with that?!

When you lose your husband, it's a nasty little secret you try to hide from friends. But eventually, they pick up on it. You can only offer lame excuses for so long when you've both been invited to dinner or a party and only one of you shows up. Eventually it becomes obvious that you've been thrown over by another.

So, if I had it to do over again, I would never have brought that d*#n widescreen TV into our home.

Alien Testing
2018

Years ago, a friend was going to visit a psychic. I decided to go too, for the adventure of it. Most of what this woman had to say seemed reasonable…even accurate…until she got to the part about alien testing.

"Have you ever noticed those tiny red spots that simply seem to appear overnight, out of nowhere? That's where aliens are performing tests. But don't worry, they're benign."

Which…the aliens or the tests?

Honestly, any credibility she might have had up until then went right out the window.

Now, all these years later, I realize she just might have been on to something. It's the only reasonable explanation I can come up with for what is happening, as I age.

This once supple body suddenly seems to be conducting sound from an alien world full of creaks and pops. Some days, it's like a virtual orchestra! I might not mind so much if they'd throw in a little real music, once in a while.

And why else would this formerly svelte figure suddenly emulate the Pillsbury Dough Boy's body on a bad bread day? Enough with the leavening agent, guys!

Then there's the issue of hair. Alien testing might just explain why hair that *wasn't* there before *is*, and hair that *was* there *isn't*. And as for that hair color testing? In my book, gray will *never* be the new black.

It also occurs to me that aliens just might be using my once-smooth skin as modeling clay. In fact, when I see the once-flawless faces of actors and musicians my age, I realize I'm not alone. It seems quite possible there's a competition as to which alien can most accurately recreate the craggy, mottled surface of their planet. Oh, we try to fight their handiwork with money and moisturizers, but believe me...the aliens are winning. It's just a matter of time.

So just think...the next time you have a bad hair day, or put on a little weight, or creak from sleeping wrong, if someone has the bad manners to comment that you seem out of sorts, you can simply say: "Alien Testing gone wrong" and walk away with satisfaction, knowing you'll leave them with a perplexed, quizzical look on their face that just might look a little bit alien itself.

This is Your Brain on Electronic Devices
2018

A study recently revealed that too much screen time has been linked to ADHD. The subject for the study was teens, ages 15 to 17. Imagine if they had studied adults who were never screenagers. I shudder to think what they'd discover screens do to the 45+ year-old mind. Visions of a frying pan with cracked eggs come to mind, along with the tagline "This is your brain on electronic devices."

Don't believe me? Why, just last week, I wanted to download one single photo from my Facebook album. A quick little task, right?

An hour and 43 minutes later, I was still on Facebook.

In fact, during that one visit, I'd ordered a licorice bouquet for a friend, learned why some people are far more appetizing to mosquitos than others, watched the latest James Corden Carpool Karaoke, bookmarked a recipe for curry-flavored mojitos, and booked a trip to Iceland, in spite of the fact that their main industry is fish processing. It must have been the promise of all that snow and ice, because *we just don't get enough* of it during winters in Rochester, NY. Or maybe it was the fact that 70% of the residents actually believe in elves. You've just *gotta* love a place like that.

But of course, I still had not downloaded my photo.

Facebook and other social media companies make money from the ads they serve up to users. Honestly, I think they'd make far more if they could figure out how to make money every time someone gets sidetracked. Yes, I mean sidetracked when using social media, but I also mean every time someone gets sidetracked when the electronic device-inspired ADHD kicks in, in real life.

Maybe you can identify with this:

Me, looking for the keys hiding in the Mariana Trench of my purse: "Oh here's the BJ's receipt I was being held ransom for at the exit...Okay, who dumped a piggy bank into the bottom of my purse? Drat, my wallet's open... Yikes! I still have to mail this check to the IRS! No wonder my bank account's not on life support yet......Ugh, purses should *not* wear red lipstick!...Tissues! Must put in tissues before movie. They should come up with a tissue rating for films....Oh no, I shouldn't have put these earrings in here! Now one's broken. Who do I know who had her nose pierced recently to give the other to?...Ah, that's where that cat toy went...."

My husband, from the other room: "Honey, you're gonna be late! Did you find your keys, or do you wanna borrow mine?"

Me: "Keys. Right. That's what I was looking for."

They'd make a fortune.

TV Hacking

2018

Have you ever noticed how domestic tasks tend to fall in the domain of one spouse or the other?

For example, I have very little to do with the electronics in our house.

There really is some upside. For example, I easily sail right past pushy sales reps in big box stores who try to run interference by asking, "Miss, do you have Direct TV?"

I bet they think I'm being sly when I respond, "I have no clue. My husband handles all things electronic in our house."

It's true, he does. And he takes great joy in playing three-card monte with the Cable, Satellite and Direct TV companies, so why should I spoil his fun?

Incidentally, those electronics that I have little to do with include the TV itself. We only have one TV in our house, and it's probably a good thing. Frustration should never be multiplied geometrically.

When I was a kid, there were only so many things you could do with a TV, once you got it. You turned it on, you changed the channel or volume, you turned it off. Now, it's more complicated than the Mars Rover. I've never figured out how my husband has all the components wired (or why we have so many components, for that matter). I asked him to write down instructions for me on how to use it. I never got past Chapter 17.

Occasionally, I experiment, just for the heck of it. In a game that feels like Russian Roulette, I sometimes find the correct remote out of the six that sit on the table next to his chair. Then, I sometimes stumble across the right one to turn on the separate sound bar. After pressing 47 buttons, if I'm lucky, I get to a screen where I have to decide whether what I want to watch is available through HDMI, PTSD, or our IRA.

Then, if by chance I *do* get to a screen that gives me all of the possible 547 options that include watching anything from TEDx to Fedex, I'm usually so exhausted I just want to take a nap.

When I can't figure it out and eventually give up, I actually take quiet solace in remembering a conversation I had about eight years ago. I was speaking with an Amish woman in Penn Yan who was showing me the dozens of stunning quilts she'd designed over the winter.

"You see," she said, "I'm really lucky not to have a TV. Look at all I get done!"

Hmmm.... Maybe I should take up quilting instead of TV hacking.

Superpowers We Could Live Without
2018

In the recently-released movie *Incredibles 2*, about a family of superpowered humans, fighting to save the world, Mom (a.k.a. Elastigirl) has been hired by a business mogul to become the PR poster child. Her job is to show the world how great superpowers are, and why the Incredibles (human beings with superpowers) should no longer be outlawed.

I really do believe most people have a superpower or two. There are just some we could probably live without.

Take X-ray vision, for example. What parent hasn't had at least one kid who could discover any birthday or Christmas gift ever bought, no matter how high-up or deviously-hidden? And as if that weren't bad enough, that same kid is usually also endowed with the ability to scale tall closets in one leap, to get them down. A package deal on those two superpowers should be outlawed.

The more I think about it, I've come to realize that X-ray vision must be a selectively-used superpower. It's really too bad it never seems to apply to finding math homework in darkened book bags or stinky gym clothes under beds.

Then there's that much-envied ability (by those of us who don't possess it) to appear and disappear at will. I don't know about you, but come Thanksgiving, I'd sure like to divest a few members of our family of their ability to appear just in time to eat, then vanish into thin air as soon as the pie is devoured, leaving clean up to everyone else. I haven't figured out how yet, but these very same people seem to have the "multiply dirty dishes geometrically" superpower as well.

Alas, none of the rest of us—tasked with cleaning up caked-on mashed potato mortar and the "motor oil" in the bottom of the turkey pan—has developed that much-envied "instant clean up" superpower.

Speaking of cleaning up, I find the "Human Tornado" superpower to be one of the most annoying. Studies show this seems to be gender-neutral, and bestowed on *at least* one member of almost every family (and woe to the family where multiple members possess this power).

Surprisingly, it appears this superpower can be used only when no one is looking. One minute, you're admiring your immaculate kitchen. The next, you walk out of the room for a micro-instant and BAM! The Human Tornado strikes!

Anyone viewing the particularly devastating aftermath of this superpower would mistake it for an especially-vicious episode of *Kitchen Wars,* where the food is winning!

The problem with these superpowers is that the people who possess them actually *use* them. With *zeal*. I can't help feeling we'd all be better off if these powers came "batteries not included."

Time Travel: Have Your Cake and...

2018

My husband likes to watch science fiction programs, which I sometimes watch with him. One sci-fi concept that simultaneously fascinates and baffles me is time travel.

From *Dr. Who* to *The Big Bang Theory*, the characters celebrate the virtues of time travel: you can go to the past and avert some terrible calamity from happening or go to the future, completely jumping over some dreadful current event. Yet in the next breath, they tell you not to mess with the time line. Heaven forbid your past youthful self sees your current present-day self!

Honestly, I'm pretty sure this wouldn't be a problem. There is no twenty-something on the face of this earth who would even *recognize* his or her middle-aged self, much less believe such a startling transformation could *possibly* happen.

Actually, I can think of a number of ways time travel could be beneficial. Take dieting, for example. You could indulge in that sinfully tempting piece of chocolate cake, then jump two days ahead. If you step on the scale and discover you've gained a pound or two as a result of eating it, you could go back 15 minutes before you ate it and refuse the serving. That way, you could have your cake and UN-eat it too!

Time travel would also be incredible when it comes to picking spouses! Imagine being able to discover whether your future in-laws are as meddling as they seem, whether your prospective spouse ever actually learns to cook or is just paying lip service, or whether your partner's charming personal quirk of "being able to sleep through anything" remains so charming when, seven years down the road, he or she is snoring soundly while you are attending to your three little children who are all up barfing at 3 am. Hmmm…come to think of it, time travel might not be so great for the institution of marriage.

Suddenly, I'm wondering if some scientist somewhere saw the risk of what could become of his or her marriage, went into the future, and UN-invented time travel.

The Kitchen Conspiracy
2018

It seems my husband and I are attracted to houses of "a certain age," if you get my drift. The centerpiece of our last kitchen was a Mary Kay pink oven, circa 1958. Alas, it thwarted my attempts to pawn it off on an antique dealer by celebrating Thanksgiving with fireworks followed by turkey tartare.

Our current kitchen is possibly five minutes newer. I don't like to brag, but enshrined on its counter is the very first microwave ever designed. Yes, my kitchen's vintage, but that's no reason for this devious obsolescence conspiracy it's plotting!

It all started with the faucet. One day it worked perfectly, the next, not. I suppose I should be grateful...some people pay a lot of money to have a fountain in their home.

That little malfunction actually saved me time in the morning. I could wash the breakfast dishes, shower, and water the plants in the hall, all with one twist of the spigot.

Annoying, but no big deal really...until I returned home from my two-hour meeting.

You just know there's a problem when you glance through the windows and see your cats perched in the chandelier. The neighbors are still referring to our house as Lake Wobegon.

The next thing to join was the microwave. Have you ever tried to open a microwave that's missing its handle? It is far easier to open a new DVD case wearing oven mitts.

Before I knew it, the dishwasher had signed on. I have to admit, it had a bit of help.

Did you know that when a 5'11" woman is surprised by an open dishwasher rack to the back of the knees, there will be ample evidence that prongs and thongs do not mix. I no longer have to mop my kitchen floor. It's now self-cleaning when we flip on the dishwasher.

Then came the burners on the stove. If you have never tried to fix a holiday dinner with only two burners and a microwave (handle attached by suncatcher suction cups), you just don't know what you're missing. It really took me back to the camping trip where I tried making spaghetti and meatballs in the rain, over a campfire, with only one pot, no colander and a palmetto leaf as a hot pad.

The most recent appliance to adopt the conspiracy was the coffee pot. Last week, for no apparent reason, the fancy schmancy carafe-less (also warranty-less) coffee maker barfed inky-colored water all over my kitchen counter that smelled like pond sludge from the Dunkin' Donuts lagoon. Thank goodness the cats tracked down its creature, as evidenced by the paw prints across our off-white carpet.

Are you seeing a pattern here? With the water I mean? My husband has seriously begun to rethink the wisdom of having married a woman born under an astrological water sign.

I've finally decided to believe that the kitchen is not really conspiring against us, it's supporting our nomination for *Extreme Makeover: Kitchen Edition.*

Nevertheless, I'm wishing I could detach the garage from our house right about now. It's a little too close to the kitchen for comfort. If the garage ever gets wind of this conspiracy, I'm afraid of the results. As a precaution, we've cut off water to that part of the house. But still, there are way too many contraptions out there that could adopt a no-blow, no-mow or no-go policy.

I'd just as soon not be nominated for CMT's new reality TV show, *Trick My Leafblower,* where they run intervention on lawn equipment gone rogue.

Helping you skate through life with a smile

It's Hard to Stay Zen in Rush Hour Traffic
2018

I admit to being a nervous driver. It started in high school when my driving instructor used to grab my clenched fist off the steering wheel to get me to relax. It's a good thing he had a brake on his side of the car too. Lampposts make peculiar hood ornaments.

Then there's the 23 years I spent in New York City, NOT driving. You don't need a car in the Big Apple. Especially in winter. I still have visions of the blizzard of '85 and shoveling out a 1960s Buick boat-of-a-car I briefly owned that a friend gave me.

As I stood thigh-deep on the snow-covered hood lifting teaspoon after teaspoon of snow off, a guy that drove by, opened his window and shouted "good luck, lady!"

He was treated to a newly-invented expletive and a sign in ASL* that has yet to be added to the Deaf dictionary.

After three parking tickets, a bout of shoveling-induced bronchitis and one dead battery, I finally had to have it towed out, and I sold that beast.

So here I am, now, in Rochester, NY where I try to avoid rush hour. People from metropolitan areas like NYC

American Sign Language

laugh at our idea of rush hour. In their minds, Rochester Rush Hour is to NYC Rush Hour as a Venus Flytrap is to Audrey II in *Little Shop of Horrors.*

What they don't realize is that the very same people who will start up a cordial conversation across the frozen foods aisle in Wegmans will pass you with vicious joy, doing 83 in a 45 mph zone.

Since sensible truck drivers avoid NYC highways like the plague, I bet most have never had the thrill of playing highway hopscotch with a truck. My personal favorite is the pickup that melts metal as the driver speeds past on the shoulder.

My husband handles all of this much better than me. I tell him that's because he missed his calling as a jet fighter pilot.

Every morning that I do have to drive during rush hour, I steel myself as I get in my car. I turn on my classical music, do deep breathing exercises and a little car yoga, and back carefully out of the drive, feeling confident, competent, and zenfully-relaxed. That usually lasts past one church, one hospital, and one Tim Hortons...until some guy runs the stop light one-half mile from our house that boasts its own 911 location code.

That's when I wonder if there's any money in publishing a dictionary of invented expletives.

Helping you skate through life with a smile

Fashion Revolution Resolution 2018

My daughters are home from college, and it's amazing what you can learn from the younger generation.

As we shared the bathroom mirror, I remarked on my daughter Danielle's clothing choice, "I didn't know you wear turtlenecks. It looks great, but I would never have thought to choose that for you."

"Mom, turtlenecks are back in style."

Back in style? I never knew they were out…or ever *in*, for that matter, unless you happened to be Steve Jobs. I just thought of them as a necessary evil. You know…for when your husband is wandering around the house in a short sleeve t-shirt while you're wearing thermal base layer, turtleneck layer, hoodie-with-hood-cinched-to-reveal-nose-only layer and furry polar bear blanket layer because, although the thermostat in the house reads 73 degrees, it *feels* like those digits are reversed.

If you talk clothing with any young-ish person, you'll discover a wealth of information. For example, the mother of one of my younger colleagues is a City of Rochester official who asked for her advice on what to wear to a gala.

"And she was going to wear *pantyhose*, for heaven's sake!" my 30-something friend exclaimed, exasperated by her mother's lack of fashion sense.

What? Not wear pantyhose? To a gala?! That's like Batman showing up at a crime scene without his cape and mask!

Out of curiosity, I sought pantyhose advice on a fashion blog. According to wardrobe consultant and blogger Hallie Abrams, it's better to go without, and absolutely necessary with open-toed shoes. She did, however, add the caveat "Princess Kate has made pantyhose cool again."

Thank you, Princess Kate, but how did I miss the memo that they're not cool to wear? It must have been sent while I was rummaging through drawers looking for my warmest turtleneck.

Blogger Hallie recommends using Sally Hansen's *Airbrush Legs* if you're too vein (pun intended) to go *au naturel*. I wonder if you can airbrush on a layer of warmth too, or are Upstate New York women relegated to wearing goose bumps and frostbite all winter?

Suddenly feeling like Downton Abbey's Dowager Countess in the age of the flapper, I decided I should, perhaps, subscribe to a fashion blog for women *d'un certain âge* (i.e., the generation that still refers to (hand)bags as purses or pocketbooks).

Do you know there are literally *thousands* of fashion blogs for women over 40, 50 and 60?! But seriously...if you're over 50, how can you trust fashion advice from someone who hasn't hit perimenopause yet? Why, she probably believes the solution to a burgeoning midriff and plantar fasciitis is fasting, sit ups, and footpads in your stilettos.

I admit that I *was* somewhat relieved that I was not alone in the fashion misfit boat, but who knew women my age needed so much help?! I found it somewhat disheartening since, once upon a time—okay, it was in my 20s—friends considered me a fashion trendsetter. Now, I feel that my entire wardrobe needs the kind of overhaul a decorator gives a haunted house.

Maybe my New Year's resolution should be to clear my closets and drawers of all vintage clothing items.

The problem with that solution is, Saran Wrap has never been my best look.

Apps of Change

2018

Just the other day, the email program I use made some darn dramatic changes. Overnight, instead of seeing my regular email dashboard, I thought I was driving a space ship.

I admit that I have a love/hate relationship with technology. It's one thing when you choose to upgrade a program. It's an altogether different animal when changes happen like an explosion, unexpectedly, and without warning.

I was talking with a friend about a recent program change where the designers hadn't quite worked out all the bugs of the beta test they'd unleashed on the world. My friend questioned whether *I* might be the one who is technology-challenged.

"Absolutely not!" I insisted indignantly. "I'm not technology challenged. I'm technology *skeptical*."

There's a difference. I prefer to have control over my chaos.

Take a minute to think about those changes to email, Facebook, Instagram, and X formerly Twitter that occur with random spontaneity. All I've got to say is that it's a really good thing the center of technology is in Silicon Valley, while most clothing designers are in New York City. The distance between them prevents these designers from lunching together every Wednesday to brainstorm new and exciting ways to baffle consumers.

Just *think* what would happen if clothing designers got the same brilliant idea as tech designers, to alter products *after* we buy them.

Just imagine walking down the street, conservatively dressed in a dapper suit and tie, on the way to an interview, when *BAM*! Suddenly, you're dressed like an extra on *Hawaii Five-O,* complete with Hawaiian shirt, Bermuda shorts and deck shoes!

Or suppose you're gliding across the dance floor, in a flattering, off-the-shoulders gown at your daughters' wedding when, *BAM*! You're clad in skin-tight *70s*-style spandex minidress, complete with white gogo boots, as if your fairy godmother is settling a vendetta!

And I won't even go into the bedlam that would break out if the car manufacturers in Detroit adopted the same strategy.

On the other hand, I might just be first in line to buy an app that worked on home décor, changing my mid-century not-so-modern dwelling into a Hawaiian coastal cabana… as long as the app also plunked it down on a secluded and palm tree-lined beach next to the Pacific Ocean.

Getting to Know You
2019

Last week, my friend Laura went to the DMV and she admitted to being "Marvelously, joyously, and necessarily surprised to have the employee there ask me for my gun permit as a form of ID."

Now, except for the curly hair, I don't see Laura as the Annie Oakley type. In fact, most would describe her as the artsy type, known for her boho attire, feather earrings, and residence in the arts district of Center City. For her to be asked for her gun permit is mildly hysterical.

The clerk then asked for her married name.

"She had a hard time taking in the notion that I could be single, to the point where she seemed to be attempting to remind me of something she was assuming I forgot."

The clerk finally indicated that if Laura didn't have a gun permit or marriage license, she was welcome to produce a truck or motorcycle license.

At this point, I was in stitches at the idea of Laura at the helm of a 16-wheeler. She drives a toy-sized car and adeptly shoehorns it into mouse-sized parking spaces.

Isn't it odd the boxes we fit ourselves into, and into which others place us, for convenience's sake? Every label…geek, nerd, prom queen, teacher's pet, star athlete…contrives to categorize us.

What if, instead of trying to categorize each other, we accept that every person is an original worth knowing?

I've found that if I take the time to really connect with someone, even people with whom I initially seem to have nothing in common, or who might initially seem intimidating or off-putting, they often turn out to be people I admire and like.

Inspired by this visit, Laura reports, "…It seems that my fear of instantaneously being pegged and dismissed as 'another bleeding-hearted-peacey-progressive-artsy-activist-npr-and-animal-loving-city-girl-at-heart type' is not warranted after all. I will now make it a point to visit the DMV more often, if only to be seen in a new light! Who knows? That motorcycle license may not be so far outside of my wheelhouse after all."

The Rage of Aquarius
2019

I was born in late January which means I'm an Aquarian. Whether or not you believe in all the astrological attributes, I can assure you that water is definitely "my sign." Since having had to be fished out of the deep end of the YWCA pool when I was five, the Water Bearer and I have had an uneasy relationship.

Take, for example, when I first began dating my, now, husband. After a lovely dinner, music and romance, we went to bed. Sometime during the night, I awoke thinking "Boy that rain's loud outside."

As I started dosing back to sleep, an insistent little voice in my head shouted, "That's not *outside,* that's *inside!*"

I jumped up, ran to the kitchen, and flicked on the light switch. Sparks illuminated the dancing waters of Bellagio's fountain cascading from my kitchen light and the roaring waters of the Niagara gushing from between the kitchen cabinets. Who expects tourist attractions so close to home?!

Moments later, the firemen showed up at my door with their axes at the ready, asking: "Miss, do you have a leak?"

"No, I have a *flood!*"

The next morning, as I was cleaning up my apartment that looked a lot like Venice, post-monsoon—thanks to a burst pipe in the apartment line—I went to put on music by which to mop. Who imagined that CD from the night before of Handel's *Water Music* would make such a great frisbee as it sailed across Brooklyn's Ocean Parkway from my fifth floor window?

Over the years, "Bridge Over Troubled Waters" has become my theme song.

As I write this, I'm waiting for the HVAC repair folks to show up. The cat pan is among the paraphernalia currently floating in the pond downstairs, thanks to a hot water heater gone rogue, encouraged no doubt, by Aquarius herself.

I really thought I'd managed to develop an uneasy truce with the Water Bearer. Apparently, the rage of Aquarius has not yet been soothed. I guess I should just consider myself fortunate not to have been born under…oh, say… a fire sign.

Helping you skate through life with a smile

Forever in Stamps

2019

My friend Elaine is like many of us…she loves to get a good deal. So when her daughter alerted her that the price of stamps was increasing on January 27, she did what any budget-conscious American who thought of it would do: she went online to the USPS site to order Forever Stamps before the price went up.

She was amazed by the selection… a veritable smorgasbord of stamps! Why, there were stamps of John Lennon, Scooby Doo, Birds in Winter, STEM Education, Sally Ride, Art of Magic, Flowers from the Garden, and even round ball stamps featuring different sports!

So, she happily clicked away, rejoicing in how much she'd be saving.

While proudly fanning her newly-acquired bouquet of stamps, she related the conversation she'd had with her husband and son upon their arrival.

Elaine to her husband: Honey, our thoughtful daughter reminded me that the price of stamps is going up, so I bought some Forever Stamps.

Husband (barely paying attention): Good idea.

Elaine: They were all so pretty, and I couldn't decide which to choose. They were at the forever price of only $.50 instead of $.55…so I bought $142 worth.

Husband (Now, definitely paying attention): You spent $142 on stamps?!!

Elaine: Well, yeah. I mean, she pointed out how smart it is to stock up now before the price goes up. And she spent $100.

Husband: But she's in a letter writing club. She mails notes and cards out almost every day! How many did you mail last month?

Elaine: Ummmm..maybe none.

Son: Mom, do you realize you just spent $142 to save $1 per book of stamps?"

It's a good thing those stamps will be valid forever, because that's how long they may last!

P.S. Elaine's motto is "I'd rather be absolutely ridiculous than boring, so, as "an angel who takes herself lightly," she gave me permission to share this true and not-even-slightly-exaggerated anecdote.

Taxing Humor
2019

In honor of tax season, and as a public service reminder of the impending April 15 ~~doom~~ deadline, I thought I'd share that I just finished my 2018 taxes.

In case you're wondering how I feel about taxes, I rank doing them right up there with, say, cleaning the cat pan. Except they take longer. Muuuuch longer. I didn't realize I'd be almost ready for social security by the time I finished.

Perhaps I misunderstood, but I thought tax reform was supposed to have made taxes *simpler* to do. I don't ever remember being asked for blood type or cup size before.

I do our family's taxes electronically, which theoretically, makes doing them easier. Digital access theoretically makes everything easier…until you actually try to gain access. You basically need the Bletchley Code Breakers to get in. It still puzzles me how hackers can tap into my accounts, but I can't. I generally have to go through about seven password changes per online visit, knowing full well that I'll have to do it again next time I log on. What I find truly ironic is when I'm asked for the most recent password I remember. If I remembered the darn password, I wouldn't be asking to change it!

Anyway, back to taxes. When my ancestors passed Lady Liberty on their way to Ellis Island and citizenship, I'm pretty sure they didn't read "Give me your tired, your poor, your *befuddled* masses…," but that could surely be the quote to apply to the ever-changing tax laws and the IRS' new empty wallet reform bill.

I still can't figure out why I spent all that time carefully logging all my consulting expenses into a spreadsheet and judiciously recording them into my online tax software, only to have it taunt "Nyah nyah nyah nyah NYAH! You can't take these itemized business deductions anymore. You have to use the standard deduction."

In the past, my bank account did a little happy dance, come tax season. This year, I'm not sure whether my pen was crying or bleeding as I wrote out that check to the IRS.

But I look at the upside.

Wait! What IS the upside?

Oh, I know! I have content for a humor column this week!

Blame It on Minute® Rice
2019

I blame it all on Minute® Rice.

I realized this fact as a guy in a pickup truck broke the sound barrier passing me on the right shoulder while I dawdled along at 63 mph in a 55 zone.

Not to point fingers, but what was Ataullah Ozai-Durrani thinking when he brought a rice cooker to the offices of General Foods, served up the very first batch of Minute Rice, and forever distorted time?

Now, 4G isn't fast enough. We need the newest 5G ultra high-fast technology, in spite of the fact that almost NOTHING is equipped to handle it yet.* But, just wait a few nano-seconds, and every company under the sun will be enticing us to upgrade our phones because, why settle for s-l-o-o-o-w service when we can have 5G?

Slow. Remember dial-up? Adds perspective, doesn't it?

Do microwave dinners take too long? Is your car self-starting so you can avoid waiting in a cold car for your auto to warm up? Does Alexa control your gadgets, saving you the time of flicking switches yourself? You may have fallen victim to the Minute® Rice Race!

Why, Minute® Rice has even influenced language. "Please wait a minute," became "Please wait a moment," and now "Hang on a sec." Who'd have thought we'd need to abbreviate the word "second?"

The faster things move, the more time-starved we are. Find yourself cramming more into every day? That makes as much sense as getting ready to pack for a trip, looking at the enormous pile of clothing you plan to take and thinking, "Oh, I better get a smaller suitcase," then doubling the amount you take!

Yup, it all started with Minute® Rice.

When I think about all those drivers that pass on a double-solid line or the shoulder because I'm driving too slowly at 8 or 10 miles over the speed limit, I take subtle delight in thinking how it must drive them bonkers each spring when they lose a *whole hour* of time, and they can't do a darn thing about it!

As we approach that day when we have to reset the clocks, I just have to point out how ironic it is that with Daylight *Saving* Time, we *lose* an hour.

Oh well, I guess we get it back every fourth Leap Year.

*Now, a mere four years later, everything is 5 G. See what I mean about how Minute® Rice has changed everything?

Animal Testing
2018

I'm going on the record to say that I'm all *for* animal testing.

What? You're offended?! Wait, you've misunderstood!

Not *that* kind of animal testing where you test products on animals! The kind where you use animals to test products! I may even start a business, using my own pets.

The first product I'll test is the bullet proof vest. I figure any vest that can withstand three assaults by a deadly cat launching itself from the floor to the middle of your chest in the middle of the night, must be bullet proof! I could even do a double trial, testing door latches at the same time, because that darn little Houdini can get through anything!

Why, I can see a whole brigade of companies lining up to use my "certified pet-tested" company! They'll start exciting new marketing campaigns!

"If our power-lift can get Bruno out of your chair, it can certainly lift you!"

Or "Hairballs versus the carpet? No sweat. Our rug shampoo will knock those spots out in the first round!" (Can't you almost hear the boxing ring bell in the background on this campaign?)

And even, "Your dog's tryst with the skunk is no challenge for our air freshener."

Why, I may have come up with my next (okay, first) multi-million-dollar business!

So if you have ideas of products I can test using my pets, send them to me, and we might both get rich!

Helping you skate through life with a smile

Grocery Shopping by Another Name
2019

Have you ever thought about how shopping for groceries resembles a hunting expedition? Instead of packing guns, hunting knives, bows and arrows, we're armed with shopping carts, reusable bags and smart phones. Laughably lethal, right? Well, if you've never been at the grocery store on Superbowl Sunday, you have no idea!

As consumers, we have developed finely-honed shopping skills that rival those of the Great White Hunter. We remember exactly where to capture our quarry, even down to the exact aisle and shelf…kind of like how our ancestors knew exactly where to find the best fish or the biggest herd of game.

But there are three scenarios that strike terror in the heart of even the most intrepid ~~hunter~~ shopper: 1) Absence of an item on our list 2) A family member's adoption of a new diet; or 3) Reorganization of the store.

Mercury must be in retrograde, because I fell victim to all three conditions this past weekend. It's really sad to see a grown woman cry in the middle of the condiments aisle.

Now, I shop at probably one of the most finely-stocked grocery stores in the entire country. And I love this store... most of the time.

But I really hate when they play three-card monte with the cereal aisle. And don't they realize how disturbing it is to find diapers where the pasta used to be? Or that putting the bulk candy where the health food aisle was is just downright diabolical?

I really wonder how many shoppers appreciate their innovative efforts to incorporate entertainment into every shopping excursion in the form of *Where's Waldo*? And what about their wisdom of turning grocery store aisles into a game of find-your-way-out-of-the-corn-maize.

Beyond the disorientation of finding yourself in a strange and looming forest of boxes, cans and jars, add the annoyance of discovering dark, cavernous hollows where a dozen items on your grocery list *used* to live. I was ready to turn in my hunting cap!

By the time I finally left the store, *Sunrise, Sunset* was the theme song for my expedition—also the length of my grocery store run. I've come to suspect that the redesign just might an experiment to test whether the amount of time spent in the store can be directly correlated with the size of the grocery bill. I have yet to disprove this theory.

Channeling Imelda Marcos
2019

They say you can tell a lot about a person by the shoes s/he wears. I surely hope not. If shoes were represented by TV shows, mine would call up images of *Golden Girls*, when, at heart, I'm really *Game of Thrones* or *Sex and the City*.

You see, I'm an Imelda Marcos wannabe.

When the Marcos' palace in the Philippines was stormed after the overthrow of Imelda's dictator husband, over 2700 pairs of shoes were found in her closet. I wouldn't really need *that* many to be happy. She had manufacturers delivering 10 pairs a *week* to her door, I'd just be satisfied if even *half* of the few shoes I have delivered *annually* didn't have to be returned. Someone should really invent a shoebox slingshot return apparatus.

My fascination with shoes started at around age 8. Then in fifth grade, just about the time I cared about what boys thought, a diagnosis of "flat feet" destined me to the triple-whammy of boy-repellants: braces, acne, *and* ugly, black, man-shoes. In despair, I greedily eyed my classmates' Keds and P.F. Flyers. Even second-hand, outdated saddle shoes seemed preferable to my clodhoppers.

I had moderate difficulty finding 11N shoes in stores throughout most of my life. Now, the internet has removed all possibility. Everyone believes "the other guy" will supply them. It's as easy to find an 11 Narrow in a store these days as it is to find a cab on New Years Eve. Even online, 11N has become as rare as a dodo bird in heels.

I long for a return to the day of the cobbler, where you'd walk in, he'd measure your feet, and you'd come back for a pair of shoes designed exactly for you! I'm seriously thinking of taking a class in shoe making. I'd design shoes for those with the wildest tastes, and only for those with the largest and smallest feet. Why, I bet even Cinderella would be forced to wear flip flops to the ball in this age of the internet.

Just this week, I saw that my friend Thomas Warfield is hosting an event as part of the Rochester Fringe Festival that's entitled "My Life with 400 Pairs of Shoes." He'll showcase his shoe collection of 40 years, sharing life and shoe stories—and he has some real sparklers, in both!

If I did a version of his show, mine would be more like Dr. Seuss' *Fox in Socks*.

Helping you skate through life with a smile

Cooking Up a Little Trouble

2019

Have you ever noticed the look in their eye when spouses approach with news they know you won't want to hear?

They have a certain walk…kind of hunkered down, like a gun slinger on Metamucil. They size you up to see if you're ready for the news (you never are), plant hands on hips, wait a moment, then shoot out, "I want to cut 50% of the meat from our diet."

This, from the man who's the poster boy for every steak house in town.

As frothy annoyance bubbles up toward anger, I excuse myself to go shower in order to keep from morphing into Ursela the Sea Witch right in front of him.

Now why does this perplex me? Because over the years, I have spent more time swapping menus for said dear husband than Chef Ramsey has spent swapping insults.

I should mention my husband's idea of cooking is popcorn. With salt. And no butter.

Okay, I exaggerate. That was pre-marriage. The occasional scrambled eggs, grits, Kraft Macaroni and Cheese, and grilled burger have since crept into his repertoire. I actually made him promise *before* we got married that he'd learn to cook at least *four* meals, so I could go out once a week without fear of our children starving.

As cascading water pummels the Sea Witch out of me, I arrive at a solution.

"So, I have a proposal," I announce, marching into the living room. "I'll make one meatless dinner per week, if you make the second. And it can't be popcorn."

To my delight, he agreed! He even began sifting through cookbooks for recipes.

Wednesday of the following week, he proudly produced an entree of eggs, grits and cheese. As we finished, he humbly noted, "This probably would have been better as a side dish."

In week two of his cooking adventure: Sweet Potato Chili. For week three: Broccoli and Tuna Casserole with Cheese. For week Four: Grilled Steak.

Happily, Ursula the Sea Witch, being unreservedly ecstatic to get a night off from cooking, didn't even tease him about the fact that the steak *looked* and *tasted* an awful lot like meat.

Cleaning Downton Abbey

2019

I really enjoyed the Downton Abbey film that was recently released. Everyone from Lady Mary to the scullery maids are preparing for the arrival of the King and Queen of England, and the estate is in an uproar!

It kind of reminds me of when my daughters return home from college with boyfriends. Spiders run for their life and places that have not seen the light of day get cleaned.

The difference is that the only servants I have to help are Mr. Clean, an assortment of emollients, and a vacuum cleaner with a wand that should really have another name. In my book, wands should simply be waved for the mess to disappear. They shouldn't be attached to a ball and chain you have to drag from room to room by a snake you have to wrestle to keep it from gobbling up tennis shoes, slippers, and the occasional cat that doesn't move fast enough.

When it comes to cleaning devices, the engineers who design them should be required to use them for a year before releasing them on the general cleaning public. I bet they'd be very different: lighter, less cumbersome….and I bet they'd have a built-in cup holder, a slot to recharge cell phones, and speakers. Who wants to whistle while you work when you can dance or sing?

Oh yes, and every vacuum should come equipped with its own light-weight, fold-out hydraulic lift that would hoist that sofa, bed or love seat right off the floor for cleaning underneath! That would solve a multitude of problems! Why, the last time I was able to vacuum under our bed, the dust bunnies had become hippos.

And how about a seat? If my neighbor can enjoy zooming around on his riding lawn mower, why can't I have the same pleasure on a vacuum? It's a similar concept, right? (Note: comments from the peanut gallery about seats on brooms and women in pointy hats will not be appreciated, even if Halloween *is* just around the corner).

If I think back to the time of Downton Abbey, I was clearly born in the wrong era. And probably the wrong class. I'm pretty sure that if anyone on the British side of my ancestry had been aristocracy, I'd know about it. Most likely, if I were part of an estate like Highclere Castle, where the fictional Downton Abbey takes place, and we were preparing for the arrival of royalty, I'd be among the household polishing silver to appoint the 120-person state dinner table, using a teensy implement not much bigger than a toothbrush, or on my hands and knees with a rag, scrubbing the floors of the 61-bedroom estate.

I guess I'll forget about time travel and stick with Mr. Clean and dragging my ball and chain around our three-bedroom "estate."

Helping you skate through life with a smile

A Lighthearted Look at AI
(Animal Intelligence)
2019

If there's one thing I've learned from isolating so long during the pandemic, it's that we've underestimated the intelligence of our pets. Who knew they only *pretend* to have the intelligence of stubborn children. In reality, they are masterminds who rule the household by domination. They carefully stalk us, watching our every move to gain power over us. We think we're playing with them, but it's *actually* the *reverse.*

Our dog Mia was still not housebroken a year-and-a-half after we got her, and I was at my wit's end. Then a pet store owner shared the trick of putting a low-hanging set of bells on the door so Mia could ring it when she wanted to go out. Within three days, the problem was solved. Since she doesn't bark, that's the tool she needed to train us to let her out.

Shortly after, our family adopted two cats whose owner had passed. I was sitting at my desk working, and I heard the bells ring quite emphatically. Did Mia have to go out *again*? I'd just let her out!

No, she was sleeping on the sofa. Did the door blow open? Did a family member come home early?

No, my little gray cat, Pepper, took a lesson out of Mia's training manual. He was sitting at the door, insistently ringing the bells, looking from me to the door to let me know he, too, wanted to go out into territory forbidden to him.

Still don't believe me on their intelligence level?

Why just this past weekend, our second cat LeeLee picked up a bottle top, brought it to my daughter's boyfriend, and taught him how to play fetch with her.

Now you may think your cat won't follow directions, or that you're teaching your dog tricks, but I assure you, they are training *YOU*. Have you ever asked a family member to bring you something rather than disturb the pet on your lap? And how often do you disrupt making your own dinner to feed the pets trolling beneath your feet? Are you pushpinned to the bed with a pet on either side, so you have to do nocturnal acrobatics just to go to the bathroom? Or maybe you have a dog who barks orders at you?

Why my sister's dog has her trained to the tone of his bark. She can distinguish when he wants to go out, when he wants her husband to sit next to her on the sofa instead of in his lounge chair, when he's demanding treats, and when he wants his daily car ride.

I tell you, we worry about AI (Artificial Intelligence), when we should really be concerned about the other AI (Animal Intelligence)! They just may take over the world.

Hmm....right about now, I'm not sure that would be a bad thing.

In Search of the Perfect Valentine's Gift
2020

I don't know how many other women have this struggle, but I often feel that it's about as easy to find a Valentine's gift for a guy as it would be to find the combination to the U.S. Treasury vault.

Most men are not easy to shop for...unless you happen to be a millionairess and can buy him a sports car, helicopter, football team, or a yacht. Tragically, I missed the big bucks boat.

Part of my challenge is that my husband is a serial hobbyist. He picks up a hobby, and I think, "Oh good! Now I'll have presents to buy him!"

Of course, once I hit the 'buy' button and those gifts and they're squirreled away in my magical gift cubby, he's on to his next hobby. Those presents are as obsolete as ice cubes in an igloo.

I've learned my lesson and did not jump on his *Queen's Gambit*-inspired chess craze. It's just as well. Without my help, he managed to acquire no less than eleven chess sets for Christmas. He now has ample-enough supply to run his own chess tournament at the next food truck rodeo... *if* he hadn't progressed to his next hobby.

So thinking about something he really enjoys, I investigated a pie-of-the-month club. Brilliant idea except that the pies were only seventeen times more expensive than making them, seven times more costly than buying them in the supermarket, and three times as much as at any self-respecting PTA fundraiser. Nevertheless, I actually briefly considered it until checkout. What they didn't warn you about is that, with each delivery, you also rent a humongous slice of the Fedex delivery truck.

Then I turned to another favorite gifting site. I feel I should warn you that if you search "gift ideas for men" on Etsy, you'll believe the only things men are interested in are T-shirts, sex, fishing, hunting, grilling, sex and knives. And did I mention sex?

Next, I went to Amazon, where I found slightly more variety. One of the first gifts that jumped out at me was a big, jerky-filled heart. Come to think of it, I've actually known a few guys who could be accused of having cornered the market on having that already.

Or how about LED flashlight gloves? Hmmm…why does *The Big Bang Theory* come to mind where short, smart, nerdy guys are dressed like superheroes pretending to shoot lasers from their fingers?

One of my favorites was the beard apron, but since my husband has never sported facial hair, the only use I could imagine this for was either a very large lobster dinner, or sloping it on to the table, and allowing small rodent-like creatures to use it as an amusement park slide. But since said rodents would be our cat's meow mix, not a five star choice in our house.

There was one additional gift I found intriguing. An Amazon #1 Best Seller in the Barware Tool Sets category were bullet-shaped cylinders that come in a circular wooden box, looking a lot like a poker chips holder, and that apparently also float in your drink once they're frozen.

They *may* also work to give guests the message that they've overstayed their welcome.

So here I am, ten days out from Valentine's Day, and still no closer than I was before the hunt to find a good gift for my guy. I guess I need to ratchet up my ingenuity quotient before I'll be able to do a Valentine's Victory lap.

Somehow, by the end of said fruitless search, I got thinking about the time in college when our French class decided to exchange Secret Santa gifts, and I pulled Professor Marceau's name.

I turned to my friend across the aisle, showed whose name I had pulled, commenting, "Uh oh. I'm in trouble."

After all, what do you get the priest who has everything?

Santa Pushed Me Off the Wagon
2020

I have a little secret I haven't liked to admit to anyone, even myself, until recently. I have an addiction.

No, not to gambling, opioids, drugs or alcohol. I'm addicted to chocolate. Okay, really, to *sweets*.

You don't know how it happens, but those caramel M&Ms, Brookside Chocolates, or Oreo cookies parachute into your shopping cart when you're not looking. Bad enough that they stow away, then they sit in your pantry singing your name, like Josh Groban crooning a personalized love song directly to you.

Of course, their siren call is the loudest at the time of day when you're most susceptible—which would be anytime—but especially after dinner when the calories can nestle all snug in your bed. Those visions of sugar plums aren't just dancing in your head, they have the run of your body, creating bowls full of jelly wherever they darn well choose.

I managed to go cold turkey on sweets about five weeks before this year's holiday season. Instead of listening to the call of Häagen-Dazs after dinner, I substituted a bowl of frozen cherries. It actually worked, without my ever having to join Chocoholics Anonymous.

Why, even at Thanksgiving when we had cheesecake, I had one small piece and didn't crave more. I swore I had my sweets craving licked, so to speak!

Then Santa pushed me off the wagon. That darn jolly old elf filled my stocking with all sorts of goodies, from chocolate covered cherries to truffles. Thinking I was in control, I had one...which became six. Before I knew it, I was slicing off slabs of Ghirardelli brownies my daughter had baked, and stockpiling Christmas cookies.

Now I know why he's so jolly...he must have very lucrative contracts with all the confectionery companies across the globe. After all, reindeer feed doesn't come cheap.

So, I'm resigned to the fact that I'm starting over. Two weeks have elapsed since the New Year and my willpower *still* hasn't kicked in. It'll probably take until Easter to break the spell again. Assuming I manage it by April, that Easter Bunny will be met with a "No Trespassing" sign on my lawn.

Confounding Google
2020

I admit to taking great pleasure in trying to confound Google. In actuality, it may be the other way around.

Out of curiosity, I looked up when Google was launched. Encyclopedia Britannica reminded me that the "American search engine company, founded in 1998 by Sergey Brin and Larry Page" is used by more than 70% of online users doing searches, and it goes on to claim that this places Google "at the heart of most Internet users' experience."

Hmmm…. I'm not sure it's the heart they're going after when those search-related products pop up as ads in my sidebar and end up choking my inbox.

I'm also not sure the way we users feel about Google has *anything* to do with the *heart*, considering the colorful language I hear floating out of colleagues' offices when I know they're using Google products.

I do worry about the fact that, in my role as a content creator for a TV station as well as a website, I do a lot of research.

Last night, for example, I asked my husband, "I wonder if Google thinks me a right-wing-radical when I search on the term Nazi?"

"I really don't think you have to worry about that. Most ultra-right-wing radicals aren't searching on terms that would define them," he assured me.

Good point.

One thing that concerns me—and my husband considered my suspicions to be conspiracy theory until last night—is how cell phones allow the "powers that be" behind ad delivery to listen in on conversations and serve up correlating ads.

If they're not listening in, how do you account for a conversation with a co-worker about Warby Parker glasses only to return to your desk to have the company's ads populating your sidebar? Or that you counter your doctor's insistence on you getting a colonscopy with an inquiry about Cologuard, only to have that little gem of an ad appear as soon as you fire up your computer?

But now, I've even got my husband convinced it's not just conspiracy theory.

We were eating pizza last night when he suddenly yelped.

"What's the matter?" I asked.

"A piece of my back tooth just broke off and I swallowed it. Dang! Now I'll need a root canal and crown. Gees, if too much is gone, I might even need a dental implant!"

Within less than one minute, an ad for dental implants popped up in the middle of the article he was reading on his computer.

You know...just because you're paranoid doesn't mean they're *not* out to target you.

A Woman's Guide to (Feeling Like You're) Losing Weight 2020

I've gained a fair amount of weight since I moved from NYC to Rochester. Well, not a *fair* amount. In my book, the fact that once women hit 40, they gain weight pretty much just by breathing is *NOT* fair at all. And once you hit 50, forget it. By that age, most women I know have tried on more diets than Elton John has tried on glasses.

The pandemic has not helped. I have this theory that calories actually float in the air like pollen. Once you add stress, monkey with sleep patterns and subtract the gym, it's the perfect formula for them to gleefully attach themselves to unsuspecting female bodies like squirrels to a bird feeder. And it doesn't help that women are often the ones making meals. I just *know* calories are absorbed through the hands.

So, I've come up with a Guide to (make you feel like you're) losing weight:

1. Never replace the battery in your digital bathroom scale. A little-known fact about digital scales is when the battery is wearing out, instead of giving you your

actual weight, they simply read "Lo." Personally, I find this a much more satisfying way to start my morning than coffee.

2. *Do NOT EVER* (yes, I'm shouting!) undertake the same diet at the same time as your male spouse/partner. They lose weight on chocolates, Cheetos® and chicken pot pies. You lose weight on…well, *air*. And *water*. Yes, on air and water you could be pretty sure to lose weight.

3. Do *NOT* buy your clothing from overseas manufacturers. Six figures are meant for salaries, not sizing. Their XXXXXL is equivalent to our size 10. And if they indicate their clothing runs true-to-size, they're referring to dolls, not humans.

4. Take a long-ish walk on a very hot day with a very slow dog that has very short legs. Your exercise app may not reflect the progress, but you'll *feel* like you've hiked the entire Sahara Desert.

As a final word of advice, *ignore* people who tell you that all you have to do is exercise *more* and eat *less*, unless they are willing to switch metabolisms with you for a month.

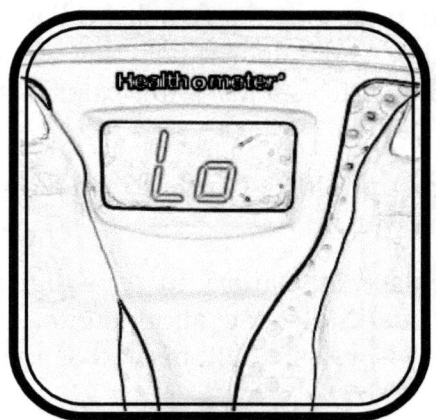

Of Cooties, Confessionals, and Igloos
2020

I have been thinking about practical solutions for dealing with the Coronavirus, especially as we begin battening down the hatches against Jack Frost.

The first idea comes from my religious upbringing. You see, I grew up Catholic, and there is one tradition I believe would be quite useful right about now: the confessional.

I'm talking about that little black box that has two human-sized, darkened compartments on either side of a wall that houses a screen through which to communicate. Traditionally used by parishioners to have contrite and penitent *tête-a-têtes* with their priests, the Coronavirus version would allow two friends or family members to have jovial heart-to-hearts without fear of exchanging convivial "cooties."

Of course, the pandemic versions will have to be retrofitted with a drain in the bottom and plastic kneelers and seats. After use, you simply hose them down and spray the screen with Lysol. I can just see it now! If my idea gains traction, instead of bake sales and craft fairs, churches can make money using a branded rent-a-confessional app! And imagine the bonus!

In one short visit, you could get a 3-C triple-header: a cootie-free Confession, Communion and Conversation, all in one visit!

While that may help with our social interactions, we also need to come up with a solution to save restaurants, because dining *en plein air* quickly loses its allure when you have to chip icicles from your nose to get the fork to your mouth.

Well, I've come up with a solution to that too! Restaurants that will be deprived of their outdoor seating options in winter can simply invest in some of those clear little plastic igloos like you see at the holiday bazaars and festivals. Up to eight could enjoy each other's company, cozied up together in an igloo, warmed by candlelight, hot food and frenzied shivering! Once the group is done, hose down the inside, put it back outside to freeze again, and any leftover cooties are trapped in pandemic permafrost.

You see…all we really need to deal with the Coronavirus is a little ingenuity! And humor. Lots of humor.

P.S. I am an "equal opportunity" humorist, so any religious irreverence is meant only to amuse, not to offend.

Where's Alice When You Need Her?
2020

You know those TV shows of the '70s? They set us up.

I bet there's not a woman of my generation out there who doesn't covet the power of B*ewitched's* Samantha, or *I Dream of Jeannie*'s femme fatale. And although magic wasn't involved, who wouldn't be delighted to welcome Alice, the funny *Brady Bunch* live-in housekeeper/cook/personal assistant/family negotiator/Jill-of-all-trades into their home?

Why, just the other weekend, my sister and I both declared almost simultaneously, "We need an Alice!"

What wouldn't we all do to have a car-driving, vacuum wielding, spatula waving sidekick who actually seems to *enjoy* taking over our most onerous and time-consuming chores that are always present, but that we don't get paid to do? Come to think of it, she *does* get paid to do them, which makes me recognize there's something definitely wrong with this picture...but that's a whole other article.

Anyway, it's no accident that Alice is at the heart of the *Brady Bunch* TV opening sequence that, in 70's clairvoyance, looks for all the world like a Zoom screen.

A friend on Facebook mentioned she'd purchased a lipstick right before the pandemic that she's never yet worn. She asked what silly things we attribute to COVID. I admitted that my excitement for the week was getting a cordless vacuum. I consider this tool my new Alice, or as close to Alice as I'll ever come. Now, *my* Alice doesn't cook, and she hasn't made me laugh...yet...but she will save me tons of time when my house starts to complain that it needs an overhaul, and there's no alternative but to oblige.

My "Alice" is a slim, lightweight model, and not really into heavy-duty jobs, but hey, if she helps lighten the load, I'm thrilled.

I do have to admit, though, that I find it sad to admit that a vacuum cleaner is my excitement for the week. Sadder still is that COVID would inspire me to use the words vacuum cleaner and excitement in the same sentence. Oh, the depths to which we sink during a pandemic!

An Electronic Symphony of Mischief

2020

Have you ever had one of those days where you feel as if every piece of technology you pick up is out to sabotage you? There's a reason for that.

Our gadgets communicate with each right under our noses, and we're not even aware of it. They act up as self-protection, just to make sure we don't get too cocky or become too efficient.

I'm convinced that, similarly to in *Peter Pan*, whenever someone says, "I don't believe in fairies" and a fairy falls down dead, whenever someone says, "I'm going off the grid," electronics everywhere malfunction in chain reaction just to remind us we really can't do that, even if we might want to.

Don't believe me? Do you really believe Siri and Google Home are there only to do your bidding. I'm sorry, but any device that can find the directions to wherever I want to go, when I can't, is highly suspect.

How else could you explain the Zoom meeting that suddenly decides to drop audio or prevent someone from joining? Or your cell phone that suddenly cuts off the call in the middle of an important interview? Or your website that crashes for no apparent reason? And how about the navigation device that keeps sending you in circles?

If this happened over a month, or even a few weeks, you wouldn't think much of it. But when these things coincide over the course of *one day*, I have to chalk it up to a scheme going on within the artificial intelligence community.

And I know darn well there's some listening device on telephone lines. How else do you explain talking to your child about her desire to study the xylophone, then having an ad for said instrument appear in a pop up when you go online two minutes later?

We think we're in control, but we're really just Mickey Mouse in a Sorcerer's pointy hat, conducting a symphony of mischief that we started when we invented the first electric light bulb.

Do I sound like a conspiracy theorist? I have a theory on that too: Just because you're paranoid doesn't mean they're not out to get you.

P.S. Just kidding...Sort of.

P.P.S. My computer just added that line, all on its own.

Who Stole My Gardening Gene?
2021

What I'd like to know is…who stole my gardening gene?

My grandfather had a lush, verdant garden that stretched on for acres. He grew so many vegetables, he had to give them away. Vegetables weren't as popular back then. His neighbors used to hide when they saw him coming.

He raised just about every variety of vegetable that could be grown in the northeast, even horseradish. As a kid, I always wondered why he'd grow that crop when no one in our family owned horses.

Then there was my father who, when he wasn't working out of town, had quite the knack for gardening. However, his outdoor plantation was no match for my mother's indoor jungle. Who knew houseplants would thrive so well in a nicotine hothouse?

As for me…even succulents beg store owners not to let me take them home. I'm probably the only person with a cactus graveyard in my window box.

Honestly, it makes me sad. At work, we were selling gardening kits as a fundraiser. I actually thought about buying one. The Master Gardeners Club formed a brigade in front of the cashier to prevent it.

I still remember fondly when my husband and I bought our first house in Sleepy Hollow, NY. I was so excited as I looked out on the back yard for the first time, imagining the beautiful terraced garden filled with roses and honeysuckle on trellises, tall glorious sunflowers, and beds of tulips, pansies, peonies and petunias cascading down the side of the hill. I quickly found out this gardener's dream was a non-gardener's nightmare. I soon had a reputation for my glorious crop of poison ivy. When my daughters went out to play, I dressed them like little hockey players, complete with knee pads and helmets to prevent contact with it.

As a gift several years ago, my friend Elaine planted a lovely magnolia tree within the stone circle in my back yard. For the first two or three years, there were glorious pink-white blooms on it. Then there were less. And less. Finally, all that was left was the bare-limbed skeleton of its former self, so my husband chopped it down. When I went out the other day to figure out what to do with the circle, now that my tree was gone, I realized I don't have to worry about that. Without even working at it, I've managed to cultivate a robust and verdant ground cover.

All I have to do now is figure out how to turn poison ivy into a cash crop, and I will corner the market.

Helping you skate through life with a smile

Designers & Dressing Rooms, Clothing & Critics
2021

This past weekend I went shopping with my daughter to help her find business casual clothing for the start of her new job.

Never mind that most clothing stores' pandemic procurements are about as exciting as an American Red Cross nurse's closet during the Korean War.

As I sat just inside the dressing room entrance, I realized this would be the catbird's seat for clothing designers, because you hear the most insightful conversations from spouses waiting outside to give a thumbs up or thumbs down to their spouse's selections.

For example, Mrs. Shopper proudly parades out of the fitting room to show her husband a pale floral cotton top, adorned with puff sleeves and ruffles at the shoulders.

"That looks like a baby's onesie top" he comments with the diplomacy of a disgruntled baseball ump.

"But, this is the latest fashion!" she protests, slinking back to the dressing room, a rookie who's just struck out.

Now, it's not just spouses who give insights on clothing design. Years ago I was shopping with my almost-four-year-old twins for a dress to wear to an elegant gala. I held high hopes as the lovely silken folds cascaded over my head and shoulders. After zipping it up, I had to admit it wasn't quite the look I had in mind. Potato sacks are seldom in style.

One of my daughters clinched it for me, "Mommy, that looks kind of *YUCKY* on you."

Kids can be the most ~~ruthless~~ candid critics.

I still remember, with some regret, how I answered my father's question about how he looked in his new outfit… gold shorts that had a blue window pane pattern and that he had paired with a solid gold, long-sleeve button down shirt, sleeves rolled up.

As the diplomatically artful preteen I was, I responded, "Dad, you look like a mustard plant."

Hey, maybe kids should take over designing clothing. I bet our selections would be far more interesting.

Casting Around for Innovation
2021

This past week, I finally got the cast off my left arm. My bright purple cast was a nasty little souvenir from my NYC trip (double entrendre intended).

Remarking to my doctor that casts have been around since the ancient Egyptians, I wondered that the medical profession couldn't come up with better advancements than neon colors and fiberglass. How about a little memory foam on the interior, for example?

"It's been the longest six months of my life," I remarked.

"You mean weeks."

"Maybe it was weeks for you, but to me, it was more like six months. Not all time is equal."

During that time, I quickly came to realize there are some things you simply *cannot* do with a cast on, and others that require innovation. For example, try explaining to your dentist how you chipped a tooth opening a Ziploc bag.

Or putting on a bra? Acrobatics and contortions like that deserve popcorn, elephants and a ringside seat. I'd ask for my husband's help, but after the second time when it took him longer than it took me, he aptly noted, "You know, we men are better at taking them *off* than putting them *on*."

And did you know that autocorrect does not work with the dictation tool to replace computer typing? It misconstrues about 20% of the words you say directly into the microphone, but picks up, with 100% accuracy, the profanity said by action figures on the TV show two rooms away. I have yet to figure out in what universe "obstacles" sounds like "testicles," but apparently, in dictationland, it does. So if you recently received any "colorful" emails from me, blame it on Microsoft.

What I really did miss was the freedom of being able to drive myself places. That L-shaped purple arm sticking out the drivers' side window at an upward right angle sent much too confusing a message when my blinker signaled a left-hand turn.

But what I did not miss at all was housework, which was almost impossible with a cast. At first, I felt a little guilty about it, until I realized that over the course of doing those chores for almost 25 years of married life, I've earned six ~~weeks~~ months off.

A Weighty Concern
2021

Have you ever noticed that between any couple, there's usually one who more easily gains, and one who more easily loses weight?

Recently, my husband has taken on the svelte appearance of his youth. I, on the other hand, could easily go as the Pillsbury Dough Girl for Halloween, especially in the aftermath of COVID (which I am sadly, this many months later, still using as an excuse). I wouldn't mind quite so much if the excess padding caused me to bounce back up when I sit down, but those darn calories seem to work in reverse, actually keeping me glued to my chair. Honestly, it's almost as if the weight my husband is shedding is planting itself on me. I've come up with a couple of theories to explain the phenomenon.

There's the distinct possibility that weight gets transferred like a cold when we kiss. Hmmm....I probably have to rule this out, or among newlyweds, one of the pair would, by default, be obese and the other, skinny as a rail.

Another possibility is that calories are conducted through the mattress at night, like electricity, from his side of the bed to mine. Could it be they prefer my side because of the extra blankets I have piled on me? Perhaps they, too, prefer the warmth.

And that's another thing! With my "extra insulation," it just adds insult to injury that my husband walks around comfortably in shirt sleeves while I'm wearing more layers than a refugee from Siberia!

Considering my husband and I have essentially the same diet, the only other thing I can conclude is that calories actually swarm, unseen, in the air! Yes, I bet that's it! Like the mosquitoes that find my husband irresistible but leave me alone, calories must have a reverse polarity to mosquitoes, preferring me to him! And because they're unseen, you can't even swat them away!

The thing is, there are lots of brands of mosquito zappers and repellants around. Whoever invents the calorie zapper will become downright rich!

Helping you skate through life with a smile

A Brand by Any Other Name Would Just Smell

2020

I remember getting into an argument with a marketing professor in grad school about what things can be branded. A commodity, he asserted, cannot be branded.

Tell that to the deodorant companies.

I had the pleasure recently of shopping for a (what…flask? Cartridge? Plastic thingy?) of my favorite deodorant.

Now I'm sure this little confession is a bit startling, but I admit to using this same brand and scent of deodorant for *years*. Tragically, and much to my chagrin, I've discovered that, these days, deodorants are pretty much like jobs. They quickly become obsolete.

So, I stood in front of a wall of 1763 deodorant choices, contemplating which should be the replacement for my Extra Dry 24-hour Invisible Solid with the Powder Scent in the 2.6 oz. size that has always lasted me 1.6 years because I don't ~~sweat~~, ~~perspire~~, glisten much.

During the past 1.6 years, the deodorant industry must have experienced a revolution. Or maybe the change has been there for a while, but I haven't noticed it before (having always been able to happily snatch my Extra Dry, in the Powder Scent off the shelf without contemplating the state of the underarm industry).

It came to me as somewhat of a surprise that the purveyors of deodorant feel obligated to sell sex appeal along with deodorant. I never thought of deodorant as a sex appeal kind of product.

Now, instead of "Powder," my underarms can smell like Cherry Mischief, Coconut Crush, or Va Va Va Voom Vanilla. I rule those out. We're talking deodorant here, not milk shakes.

I also rule out Himalayan Sea Salt, Oars & Alps, Caribbean Cool and anything else that sounds like my underarms will have more fun than I do.

When my eyes hit the men's row, I discover the names that apparently appeal to men all have phallic symbolism... Alpine Force, Cool Peak, Pacific Surge, or Urge.

They've even come out with line extensions of deodorants just for Teens. What self-respecting teenage girl wouldn't want to apply a deodorant with the name of Selfie Stick, Pool Party, or Pink Crush to her underarm, especially since that last is described as "cute and girlie?" What I'd really like to know is: since when has cute become a descriptor for an underarm? Or a deodorant, for that matter?

The whole shopping adventure starts me wondering if deodorants that don't have exotic names *even work*. Maybe some of them won't work for *me*, because I'm not their target audience? After all, the description for Pink Crush says, "The harder you play, the harder it works!" It's been a while since I've played really hard…maybe the 1st grade playground…so, a few decades, give or take.

After pacing the length of the aisle at least fourteen times, I leave the store empty-handed feeling dazed.

It's a good thing deodorant companies don't have a truth-in-selling policy, or those deodorants targeted at women *d'un certain âge* (like yours truly) would be sporting names like "Hot Mama in More Ways than One," "Don't Be Deceived, I'm 32 at Heart." or "Granny to the Stars."

The Gnomes of Status Quo
2022

Have you ever noticed how status quo fights against change? Like a stubborn, naughty gnome, Status Quo stamps his tiny feet demanding *NO* change.

I've often encountered these annoying little creatures, but recently they have persistently appeared in three areas of my life: the junk mail stack, the bathroom scale, and family Christmas traditions.

If you have ever tried to eliminate the junk mail pile that magically forms on your counter like mold on an excavation from the back of the refrigerator, you'll understand what I mean. The Status Quo Gnome is bound and determined there should be no empty counter space. And if you do manage to banish that pile from one place, it materializes elsewhere as a veritable leaning tower of junk mail.

Then there's the bathroom scale. Just about the time I think I've mastered my new eating lifestyle, and the numbers on my scale have begun to descend respectably and consistently, the Status Quo Gnome (also known in diet circles as the Set Point Elf) wakes up from his nap. I now find myself on the opposite side of a seesaw from this little rascal. For every .2 of a pound I manage to shed, that little tormentor wants to tack on .4 of a pound, in retribution for my trying to make a change.

Especially perplexing at this time of year is the Status Quo Gnome of Christmas traditions past. This wee character is apparently also a politician, coercing others to lobby on his behalf.

This year, I decided to pare down and change up our normal Christmas traditions. Suddenly, real and (perhaps) imagined voices pop up saying, "What? You're not putting Santa on the mantle?" "Oh, but you've got to put up lights on the house, or it won't be Christmas," and "How can you even *think* of not baking homemade Christmas cookies?" (I'm pretty sure this last comment was made by the Set Point Elf disguising his voice as a family member).

I think I just figured out a way to get even! Ha! For all those times I don't get around to something…for example, the year the Christmas tree stayed up until Valentine's Day, or the dishes sat in the sink overnight, or I skipped grocery shopping for two weeks, I can simply say, "The Gnomes made me *NOT* do it!"

Helping you skate through life with a smile

Inheriting Up
2022

Many people *d'un certain âge* aren't thrilled when they have to help clean out their parents' home as Mom and Dad downsize, move into a smaller retirement bungalow, or more sadly. pass away.

"You wouldn't believe the crap they've saved over the years," their kids shudder. "It's like they can't get rid of *anything!*"

I've recently been thinking about this phenomenon, based on my daughters moving along in their own lives—graduating college, getting exciting new jobs, moving to apartments in distant cities....

Oddly, and almost simultaneously, the house my husband and I bought 16 years ago looks like it's bursting at the seams, or like an unusual type of flood went through, leaving tons of debris but washing away the flood's physical damage and watermarks.

Which brings me back to the fact that, if those people my age looked closely at the flotsam and jetsam they're clearing out of their parents' homes, it just might look vaguely and disquietingly familiar.

For example, I look at the banana hanger with the cute little monkey propping up the hook and think, "I didn't buy that. When did that show up?"

Then I remember one daughter's roommate's favorite fruit was bananas. Aha! Mystery solved.

I discover there's a whole box of lovely blue and white dishes squirreled away in the garage that were never my husbands' and mine, and that we didn't inherit from either set of our parents. As I stare at the pattern, I vaguely, then fondly, remember a thrifting expedition for one daughter's kitchen, when she moved into her first apartment off campus.

I soon begin to wonder if toy manufacturers even realize their Lego® toys, Webkinz and Beanie Babies have such long half-lives. As proof, I can show them 1,397 stuffed animals, scrupulously sealed into vacuum-packed plastic bags, and stacked in our basement, secretly plotting their own *Toy Story*, in revenge.

Who knew when you become a parent, you eventually inherit up?

So the question becomes, why don't we get rid of the stuff our children pass on to us?

I can tell you why. You see...parents walk a very fine line between, "Mom, why would you ever think I would want those books again," and "Mom, why did you get rid of them? I wanted those books for my daughter when I have one!"

With the choice of annoying your kids or depriving your grandchildren, who would ever deny their children the privilege of rummaging through the flotsam and jetsam of their youth?

Helping you skate through life with a smile

Searching for the Bermuda Triangle
2022

Do you remember hearing a lot about the Bermuda Triangle some years back? The Bermuda Triangle is that oddly-shaped region of the Atlantic that sits between Miami, Florida, San Juan, Puerto Rico, and Bermuda.

Conspiracy theorists have many ideas about how whole planes, boats and even people have disappeared in this region. Some credit extraterrestrials, others attribute it to the influence of the lost continent of Atlantis, still others assert vortices suck objects into other dimensions.

Scientists generally attribute the disappearances to inclement weather.

If you haven't heard much about it recently, there's a reason: It migrated. It now hovers over our home. That is the only possible explanation I can find for the fact that so many items in our home have gone missing.

Oh, you expect the occasional half pair of earrings to disappear, and there's always that black hole in the dryer that swallows entire socks, but far more has gone on recently that is truly inexplicable.

I went to make the bed this week with my favorite set of soft flannel snowflake sheets, and they were *nowhere* to be found. I checked every cabinet, chest of drawers and closet where they would likely have been put. You just *know* I'm desperate when I clean out three closets, the dog's chest, and throw out half of an entire linen closet in search of them!

Then, there are the lighted Moravian stars we bought to put in the the windows at Christmas last year. Poof! Gone! My husband swears he put them in a safe place where we could find them this year, but after a search that would put Scotland Yard to shame, I have to believe they have fallen victim to our own personal Bermuda Triangle.

What really concerns me is that this green-eyed triangular monster is becoming more aggressively voracious over time! It has already swallowed the waterproof moleskin cap that I gave my husband for Christmas, a corkscrew, a case of wine, a Father's Day gift, three cook books, my husband's blood pressure apparatus, a pair of shoes, and probably a number of items that we haven't missed yet... all gone, into the belly of this beast.

Now, if we could just figure out a way to get all the stuff we *don't* want and need to fall into that Bermuda Triangle, we could cancel our appointment with 1 800-GOT-JUNK.

Clothing Revenge

2022

Have you ever gotten ready for work, church, or to go out to dinner, and discovered that, as much as you may want to go, your clothing doesn't?

If you regularly try on more than, say, four outfits before you find one that works, you know what I'm talking about.

I swear that the clothes in my closet draw straws to choose which outfit will be forced to go, and which ones get to relax all day in the closet. I think they even swipe each other's wrinkles, just to avoid being trotted out, because by now, they all know darn well that my iron is on permanent R & R in an asylum somewhere. A few adventurous items have even gone so far as to fling themselves to the floor in petulance, letting the cat sleep on them, to avoid being worn. Others hide so far back in the closet, they go undetected for years. By the time I find them, they've shrunken so badly from lack of light and air, they fit like… well, they just don't, even if they *have* come back in style.

I really don't think I'm imagining this. How else could you explain the sweater that used to fit sveltely, but now sports a bustle in the back or a faux baby bump up front? Or the button-down shirt whose collar stands up so straight it puts nehru jackets from the '60s to shame? Then there's those pants with the hem sporting a snarl of thread that looks like Christmas tree lights gone awry.

But little do they know, I now have a secret weapon! It's called dress-down day. Where I work, about twice a month, we can basically wear whatever we want, without regard for conformism, fashion, or convention. It's all about convenience and comfort.

So now, if my clothes start throwing temper tantrums, I will give them a time out for a day or two, then force them out on dress down day! Ha! Take that, you misbehaving clothing! Revenge is a plate best served wrinkled!

Helping you skate through life with a smile

Measuring Pandemic Clutter
2022

I wonder how many other families out there have ended up with a cache of clutter courtesy of Amazon and the pandemic?

In the past two years, our family's clutter factor expanded exponentially. The question is: Now what?!

One of my "favorite" acquisitions is the collection of slide rules my husbanded decided he desperately needed to measure…what? The hours of boredom in a pandemic?

In case you're wondering about the function of a slide rule, I had only the vaguest notion, so I looked it up. It's a "mechanical analog computer." No, not the kind you tap numbers into in order to calculate fuel costs and mileage, budgets, or how many calories you're over your daily diet allotment. It's the kind that looks like one ruler embedded in another, where you slide the two parts back and forth to perform mathematical wizardry. If only that wizardry worked to reduce taxes!

Alas, in school, I was born too late for slide rules, and too early for computers. No wonder I was abysmal at math.

Anyway, when I think of slide rules, I think of Katherine Johnson of *Hidden Figures* fame, computing John Glenn's trajectory of the Friendship 7 capsule. In truth, she may have been so brilliant, she didn't need a slide rule.

But back to my husband's collection. I think we now have enough slide rule power to chart our way to Pluto and back. In the event NASA does not need my husband to navigate to the farthest no-longer-planet in our solar system, we could always open a museum. Hey, if the JELL-O museum in Leroy, NY has had success, maybe one for slide rules could be a hit, especially if we add amusement park rides, vintage rock music and an adjacent home-style diner that serves booze in tall glasses, the quantity of which would be measured by slide rule scale.

In frustration over the burgeoning collection of antiquated measuring tools piling up in a chest in our bedroom, I ~~complained~~ commented, "There must be $500 worth of slide rules in those drawers!"

He countered: "Oh, I'm sure there's *a lot more* than that."

I couldn't help but notice the slightly self-satisfied look on his face.

For lack of a better option, I choose to look on the bright side. If the cost of fuel keeps going up, we now have ample supply of kindling, albeit, valued at only slightly less than what the fuel would cost.

I also have to take satisfaction in knowing that if any scientists ever want to measure the amount of clutter caused by the pandemic, we can provide them with lots of the perfect measuring tools!

Coming Back as a Classy Chassis
2023

I think in my next life, I'd like to come back as a slick, sleek automobile.

I decided this when I tried to get a checkup with my primary care physician last week. Right after calling my GP's office, I called my car dealership for ~~a check-up~~ an inspection for my car. How does my car rate Wednesday, but I rate October?

I've thought about the many advantages to being a car. For example, I'd never have trouble finding the right size ~~shoes~~ tires. I wouldn't even have to order them online from galaxies far, far away, as I do my shoes. And while they might cost somewhat more, I don't know of many pairs of shoes, even sneakers, that are still going strong after 50,000 miles.

And think about this: a car can guzzle as much fuel as it can hold without A) weight gain, B) multiple trips to the rest room, C) inebriation, or D) a hangover. Can you boast that?

A car never worries about what it will be "when it grows up," where it will find its next job, or whether it will have enough money to retire.

Another upside is that most cars get plenty of love and attention. I know of some cars whose owners spend more time with their autos than with their spouses. Come to think of it, in many of those cases, it's probably just as well.

The only downside I can think of is that, as a car, you would be stuck with your styling. Heaven forbid that, in your next life, you come back as a futuristic chartreuse AMC Gremlin, to forever be classified by auto aficionados as one of the most ugly cars ever made...the outcast of the auto world!

Oh, don't get the idea that I'm complaining about my "current model." My upholstery may be a little overstuffed these days, it's got a fair number of miles on it, and the engine's not quite as spunky as it used to be, but this classy chassis has taken me on plenty of fabulous road trips and fine adventures! If I get to come back, I just hope the next one is as good!

Helping you skate through life with a smile

Communication Discombobulation

2022

Every night that my Dad wasn't working out of town, at 6 pm, like clockwork, he sat down in his favorite chair to watch the local news delivered by journalist Fred Hillegas. I grew up watching that dour journalist deliver news of fires and bank robberies, Viet Nam and Watergate in deadpan black and white. The concept of an upbeat story at the end of the broadcast didn't exist. In those days, we had little choice. There were three TV channels, and we were lucky to have a TV. Many people didn't. My friend Rupert jokes that his parents stopped having kids—he's the third of eight—when they got their first TV.

Today, we're buffeted with a frenzy of choices…so many, in fact that I bet you've had that unsettling feeling of communication discombobulation…of having seen something you want to share with someone—a cartoon, recipe, meme, photo or article—but you have no idea where you saw it. Was it on a website, in a book, magazine or newspaper, on Facebook, Instagram, Twitter or LinkedIn, on Reddit, in an email, a text or in messenger?

It's all the more disturbing when it's something that came in for work, and it is a document that you should have saved, but didn't. Was it in an email, a text, a Google doc, and heaven forbid, did it come as an attachment? It's like chasing a kite in a tornado.

Honestly, there's a sliver of my brain that's turning to pie from trying to remember where, in all the possible choices, I found that crust of information.

There's also the pressure of remembering the best way to communicate with each individual. Is it a phone call, by text, in an email or via Messenger, Zoom, through Linkedin, or Google Meetup? And depending on what tool is optimal, you also have to remember the unstated rules of that tool. I sent a text to a friend early in the morning—because that's when I thought to send it—and I was good humoredly chastised for weeks about not following the rules of etiquette for texting. Who knew there were texting rules…for an application where you ignore punctuation and abbreviate entire words with nonsensical letters?

Some company could make a fortune creating an app that helps people avoid communication discombobulation by tracking their communication trail.

Of course, the only problem is that you'd have to remember whether you'd installed it on your work phone, your cell phone, your work computer, your home computer, your iPad, your tablet, your [fill in the blank with the next tool that comes along].

And once you remember that, how will you remember which communication apps it even tracks?!

Kitchen Capers
2022

Have you ever noticed that when you put something into the refrigerator, it somehow multiplies? One leftover pasta dinner that got lost in the back turns into seven dirty dishes. It's true! Why, I bet whoever invented the refrigerator didn't know it had magical powers to transform perfectly edible meals into brightly-colored science experiments that could fuel a kaleidoscope or win a science project award.

Now that there are only two of us in the house to chip away at the leftover lineup, our refrigerator refuse has grown geometrically.

Why just last weekend, my husband discarded a fine collection of mold-laced cheeses. When my daughters were living at home, cheese slices raced to become grilled cheese sandwiches, and no muenster would live long enough to rival Shrek.

Now, we have a scientist's dream stash of live growth petri dishes lining our refrigerator shelves.

Oh, I try to cook reasonable amounts, but it's hard to downsize from 15 meals a day—3 for every person in the house during the pandemic when everyone was home, including a Brazilian boyfriend—to 1 evening meal each for my husband and me. I wonder if mess hall Sergeants have this challenge when they return home on leave to cook for their family?

Wouldn't it be great if there were a market in the world of science for refrigerator leftovers? Imagine if the mold from leftovers could be converted into medicine and save the world from maladies like COVID, polio, monkeypox and the flu. Or better yet, suppose it could be converted into renewable clean energy to fuel vehicles of all sorts?!

Why, over the course of a year, I bet we could collect and recycle enough refrigerator refuse to power the International Space Station! That would be one small step for the Llewellyn household, one giant leap for mankind!

Reclaiming Pandora's ~~Box~~ Closet
2023

It's a little known fact that does not appear in the media, but right now, in homes all across America, Pandora has taken over entire closets. Never mind the tiny boxes this woman from Greek mythology utilized to release evils on the world. Now, she's gone big time.

I share advice with anyone tasked with the unpleasant task of cleaning up Pandora's mess.

First, you'll have no clue what you may find there, so go as prepared as a lion tamer entering the circus ring. This takes both physical and psychological strength.

Instead of breeches, red buttoned coat, top hat and whip, arm yourself with step stool, apron, hair covering and rubber gloves. Boots are optional, and gas mask may be advised if it's a child's room. I still remember the potato salad my sister and her friend stowed for safe keeping one New Year's Eve, that was sniffed out weeks later, mistaken for a dead rodent.

Stock up on ironclad trash bags, indestructible boxes for Good Will, and milk crates or other containers to organize the fiasco. Pandora cannot thrive in an organized environment.

Then, send the family away, set aside an entire weekend, and blast some very good music by which to clean. Also remember: clutter expands exponentially the deeper you dig, so be prepared with my mother's mantra, "It gets worse before it will get better."

The last time I purged Pandora, among the "treasures" she had hidden in our blue laundry room closets were Candyland (our daughters are 22), some of the first light bulbs invented by Edison that fit none of our lamps, and a tabletop loom I bought just out of college. Also found: the emergency kit my husband put together the week after 9/11. Hmmm, I wonder…do vacuum-sealed space foods have a shelf life?

My final piece of advice is, when you finish cleaning Pandora's closet, store your favorite beverage in the back for the *next* time you're inspired to Purge Pandora.

Alas, you will have to do it again, because once Pandora has found a home in your closet, she will re-invade like wasps to a hive. Depending on whether or not your family members are enablers, her reinvasion may take less time than you might expect.

As for the beverage of choice, if you think you'll be purging again within the next five to ten years, vintners recommend vintage champagne as a good choice. On the other hand, if your family members are more conservative at assisting Pandora, fine wine makes more sense, since it can last up to 10 or 20 years.

If your family is as good at enabling Pandora as mine, Kool-Aid in a zip lock might be just about right.

Déjà Vu, All Over Again
2022

Now that the mid-term elections are (sort of) in the rearview mirror, can I just say I'm not a fan of political ads?

Political ads tend to extoll the effectiveness of their candidate, warn of the pitfalls of going with competitors, overemphasize dangers, overpromise on results, and drive fear mongering based on "what ifs…."

They also seem to have an unsettling lack of truthful information on which to make an informed decision.

If you go with their candidate, they promise health, wellness, and happiness. Go with the competitor, and the consequences are dire! Your once calm, complacent life is going to turn into Nightmare on Elm Street. Or worse.

I was actually happy to watch TV on Wednesday night and not see one single political commercial. Their absence did *not* bother me one iota. It was back to the traditional lineup of pharmaceutical ads.

And then, as I watched one pharmaceutical commercial after the other, I had a distinct feeling of déjà vu. Have you ever stopped to think about how much political ads emulate pharmaceutical commercials?

Can I just say I'm not a fan of pharmaceutical ads?

Pharmaceutical ads tend to extoll the effectiveness of their medication, warn of the pitfalls of going with competitors, overemphasize dangers, overpromise on results, and drive fear mongering based on "what ifs...."

One undeniable difference is political ads warn of potential devastation to the country while pharmaceutical ads warn of potential devastation to the body.

Who knew that to create political or pharma ads, all you have to do is switch out the words in the descriptions of outcome and images of product for political or pharma ad success?! I bet politicians and big pharma could save big bucks if they just shared the same ad agency!

Collaborating with Artificial Intelligence 2023

Twice this past week, I've received entreaties out of the blue to collaborate on an AI-powered article. I was surprised that I was "one of a few experts invited to add" my expertise on the topic of coping with creative blocks in writing press releases. The writing of this article had been started by Artificial Intelligence.

Wait! What? I'm supposed to help Artificial Intelligence write an article? I could have sworn it's supposed to work the other way around.

And I didn't even realize I've ever had to cope with a creative block in writing press releases. This was news to me.

The more I think about this invitation, the more I've wondered if *anyone* would feel flattered to be one of "the few experts" selected to collaborate, pro bono, with AI?

I wonder…how does artificial intelligence even determine on which subjects we're experts? I'm almost afraid to ask. Does it cull through our online resumes and profiles? Maybe it uses ChatGPT to converse with our employers or loved ones to discover what they perceive as our "strengths."

I know a few people who might be embarrassed if certain "talents" ever got out. Nobody really wants the world to know they can finish off a gallon of ice cream in one sitting, comfortably go a week without taking a shower, or that they know every Sesame Street song by heart.

I find that I'm actually a little insulted by the invitation. As if I would help AI write articles in the pursuit of teaching it to take over someone's job...as many fear.

On the other hand, I (and probably a lot of other people) would be happy to collaborate with AI on writing articles on the topics of lawncare, housecleaning, filing taxes, and changing diapers, if Artificial Intelligence would actually *take over doing* those jobs.

Travel Tribulations
2023

Years ago, I heard an anecdote about a man who walked up to an airline check-in desk and asked the clerk to send one bag to Ft. Myers, one to Baltimore Washington International, and one to Rochester.

The clerk was scandalized. "Sir, we can't do that!"

"Why not? You did it last time."

When I first heard that tale, I was amused. I never dreamed that bag would be *me* one day.

Recently, my husband and I flew from Denver to Rochester, NY by way of Ft. Myers, FL , then Baltimore/Washington International. Eighteen hours of transit, for what should/could have been a 4-hour direct flight. Stagecoach might have been faster.

Somehow, I lowered my guard at the promise of "only one transfer," not realizing they super-glue you to the seat in Denver to distract you from the fact that your final destination doesn't even have palm trees and drinks with little umbrellas.

There's no doubt that travel has gotten more challenging. At TSA, you are required to remove so many things these days that it surprises me you're still allowed to keep your underwear on.

On one particular airline, your bag flies free, but you have *no reserved seat*. It was so crowded, I was thankful there is no longer a middle ashtray, because I was pretty sure someone would have been seated in it.

After my recent travels, I have a word of advice: no matter how short your advertised flight is, pack food. And drink. And lots of it. Seriously. For the length of trip we had, you'd have to down every mini pretzel packet on the plane to even *activate* your diet app.

In December, my husband and I are supposed to visit our daughter in Sweden for Christmas. Travel is still four months away, yet two legs of our four flights have already been cancelled and rescheduled twice.

I'd just like to understand how they know in March that in December 1) the weather will be too lousy to fly, 2) there won't be enough pilots or flight attendants to manage the flight, or 3) there won't be enough passengers to fill those ashtray seats.

When I was younger, I fantasized about having the wherewithal to pack a bag, go to the airport, and decide my destination based on what location struck my fancy. Now, I'd just be happy with a direct flight.

Of Ovens and Athletes

2024

Our oven has been on strike this past couple of weeks, spitting out only half-heartedly-cooked meals.

I've come to realize that ovens are like athletes: you need to give them time to warm up, and once they get past their prime, it's time for retirement.

At first, I thought I hadn't given my vintage warrior a sufficient pep talk or enough warm up time, causing my brownies to come out the consistency of a mud bath.

So, rather than simply throwing in the towel on our antique athlete who has given us many great years of winning meals, I went out and purchased an oven thermometer.

That night, I set the oven to 400° to cook clam strips, and I waited ten minutes. Alas, a cool 0° on the thermometer confirmed the sad news that my antique athlete had definitively kicked the bucket.

As I contemplated how to healthily cook clam strips, without oven or air fryer, I commented to my husband, "Well, our oven is officially dead. We're going to have to look for a new one."

He responded, "Do we have anything planned for Saturday?"

Me: "Not that I know of, why?"

Him: "Because I'm making an appointment to give blood."

Wondering what giving blood had to do with my culinary conundrum, I replied "I thought you were asking so we could go look for a new stove."

Him: "Memorial Day Sales are coming up."

"It's March 8th. Memorial Day isn't until May 31st."

Him: "Well, we don't use the oven that much, do we?"

I was *almost* able to bite back the words, "Well, one-half of 'we' never uses it."

On Saturday, the situation was still status quo when I asked him what he might want me to pick up at the grocery store.

"Do they have any cinnamon buns?"

Hoping he would ask for something like that, I responded, "They do. In a pop-open container by Pillsbury. Unfortunately, I can't make them, because this half of 'we' needs an oven to do so."

I can't help but think that if that darned oven had a pull cord or starter button, we'd have gone out the very night it broke to buy a new one.

P.S. Beware of annoying the writer. You may find yourself the subject of a humor column.

Extreme Travel Packing 2024

I love to travel, but I'm not a big fan of packing. Come to think of it, I don't know many who enjoy it.

I usually wait until the night before the trip, take out my packing list, and throw the stuff on it into a bag. I use the list as insurance against last minute packing errors, after having forgotten underwear and birth control once too often when I was younger. The underwear you can live without, or replace almost anyplace. Having a prescription transferred across state lines is like trying to smuggle a watermelon out of the supermarket under your t-shirt.

I think most people take a "middle of the road" approach to packing but I could be wrong. Two members of my own family lead me to think extreme packing is more common than you might think.

My sister likes to pack 63 days in advance.

Have you ever seen one of those old westerns where a woman is visiting family "out west" and arrives by sagging stage coach laden with her 17 bursting-at-the-seams steamer trunks and 14 pregnant carpet bags? That would be my sister…for a long weekend. Hers is the first dog I know who arrives with his own pair of matching steamer trunks.

My friend Rupe talks about their four-hour picnic packing expedition when he went to visit her. The table was overflowing with at least two options of every condiment known to man, five choices of bread, seven choices each of cheese and cold cuts, four chip choices, a fly swatter, two scents of bug repellant, three types of sunscreens, two different shapes of ice, a convenience store's selection of drinks, and a 500-pack of paper plates. She gracefully wedged everything into three coolers that made the back of their RV sag.

"And do you know what?" He exclaimed in disbelief. "We used every darn thing."

My husband is soon having surgery for which my sister and daughter are both, kindly and generously, coming in for moral support.

My plan was to bring a book and hit the cafeteria for lunch. I was surprised to learn they had developed plans to put together a 'to-go bag' to get us through the multi-hour surgery.

Upon hearing its contents, I've hired a dog sled to get it to the hospital. I wonder if sled dogs are considered service animals?

Almost every game known to man will be in it, along with a tablet loaded with every Oscar-winning film since 1929. We've been scheduled to read a book in advance so we can discuss all 553 pages. In case of hunger or thirst, break glass on the bag's produce stand and tea shop.

I can't help but compare that to my other twin daughter's boyfriend, Eric. She and he have headed to Japan and South Korea for three weeks. His lunchbox-size backpack has three t-shirts, two pairs of shorts, ample underwear, and his smart phone that serves as GPS, entertainment console, camera, travel planner and communication device.

My husband tends to fall into the Eric mode of packing.

When I shared this comparison with my friend Donna, she said, "I'm definitely in your sister's camp."

Apparently, when her daughters were in field hockey, she was known as "Mrs. Golashes," acquiring that name because her suburban was so well-stocked, with four season's worth of clothing in multiple layers, including footwear for every occasion, a BJs stockpile of granola bars and sports drinks, and a pharmacy's supply of medical and feminine hygiene products.

Hmmmm.... If you think of the bell curve of extreme travel packing, where my sister and friend Donna are on one end, my husband and Eric are on the other, and I am in the middle, *I* may be the odd woman out.

Helping you skate through life with a smile

The Ants Go Marching...
2024

We seem to have a serious ant problem this year. No, not the kind in the clever Geico commercial that uses the homophone about annoying female relatives telling you the contents of your fridge has expired, the annoying ones that traipse across anything that's not moving. Beware sleeping pets and snoozing spouses!

In a kind-hearted gesture, I trapped the first few in a glass and moved them outside. I didn't put tracking tags on them, but I'm pretty sure those same exact little suckers came back for seconds and thirds. So I've had to resort to more drastic measures.

To "invite" them to depart from our premises, I purchased a case of ant bait. The instructions assured me that the little critters take the poison back home, thereby killing the entire colony. I suspect the ants are too smart for that. Instead, the colony hears the ant with the poison picnic coming, and they all stampede in ~~a beeline~~ an antline straight to our house to escape.

I proposed the idea to my husband of putting a sugar lick in the yard, similar to salt licks for deer, to keep the ants outside, but he assured me this would only ensure more would visit, leaving little sticky (Paw? Foot? Leg?) prints on every surface. I ditched that idea.

But now, the problem has magnified. As I was doing research on one computer monitor, out of the corner of my eye, I caught the cursor on my other monitor moving all by itself. Shifting my gaze to the second screen, I was horrified to realize that if that ant-disguised-as-cursor had his way, he'd be editing my text.

So my husband went out and bought a pack of ant traps to put on the *exterior* of the house, and those seem to be helping.

All I've got to say is, lucky for the ants that we're low on chocolate right now, or I might be tempted to see if I have the "refined and adventurous palate" (description courtesy of Amazon) that might allow me to enjoy these "chocolate covered delicacies."

In a slight twist of idiom, I say, "If you can't beat'em, eat 'em!"

Helping you skate through life with a smile

Driving the Prom Queen
2024

I own a beautiful white and black 2020 Nissan Kicks. I bought her certified pre-owned in early 2021 with a mere 354 miles on her because she had been sitting on a car rental lot, bored to tears during the pandemic, watching traffic <u>not</u> go by. I am sure the rental agency sent her to the dealership just to socialize her with other cars, and make sure she still remembered how to be driven.

She and I bonded, friends right from the first drive. The problem was, the guy who test drove her right before me decided *he* wanted her. I was ready to walk off the lot empty-handed, since I had my heart set on her, but then the sales rep persuaded the guy that the bright red, revved-up, option-stacked model was made for him. Fate had spoken!

Last month, I had her in for her yearly inspection, and she was in prom queen condition. She has only slightly over 26,000 miles on her and she's pristine.

But now I have a problem. The dealership wants her back. In fact, every dealership in town seems to desire her.

Upon my return from the inspection, I had barely gotten her into our garage before one of their sales reps called, telling me he could take her off my hands, because they need cars like her.

Now this was not the first or last proposal I'd received. I've had post cards from other dealers, plus my dealer has sent me one or two snail mail flyers, a couple of emails and several texts wanting to reclaim her. My favorite was the invitation for *the two of us* to attend a *reception* where I could upgrade her to the auto of my choice.

They explained that she was such a beauty, they would be happy to buy out my contract and I could end up with lower monthly payments if I upgraded her.

What kind of friend do they think I am?! Do they think I'm so disloyal that I'd turn in my BFF for a newer, shinier model just as she's starting to gracefully age?!!

There have been a constant barrage of proposals. I finally tested the intent of the last guy who called, saying that the only way I'd consider trading her in is if they <u>*gave*</u> me, no fees attached, a *brand-new model of my choice.*

It turns out, that's a *great* way to get a sale rep off the phone.

I guess even the Prom Queen doesn't merit that level of ~~bribe~~ incentive.

A Finite Art
2024

Have you ever noticed that when you do something on a regular basis, you develop your own process for doing it? You take an everyday, mundane task that you are required to do on a regular basis and make it your own. Heaven forbid someone else takes over your task and they choose to do it differently!

I first noticed this phenomenon when I volunteered one summer as a counselor at a camp at which my daughters got to learn about and ride horses. In addition to being the Counselor for Arts and Crafts, I ~~slaved away~~ helped in the kitchen for breakfast, lunch and dinner.

Thinking about the camp's kitchen manager this many years later, I'm certain her blood pressure numbers exceeded those on the deep fryer. Rumor has it that when the camp closed for the season, she taught Drill Sergeant Camp for the Army.

For lunch one day, I was asked to mix the Kool-Aid, considered by the camp to be the breakfast, lunch and dinner drink of champions. This seemed like an easy task.

1) Take pitcher from shelf.

2) Add prescribed amount of powdered lemon Kool-Aid.

3) *"STOP!" s*creeched Sarge.

"Carol, you've added *way* too much mix! Do you think this camp is made of money? Use *a third* of that!" Sarge shouted.

3B) Dump two-thirds of mix back in powder container.

4) Add water, diluting Kool-Aid to the color of…well, use your imagination.

5) Mix until… *"HALT!"*

"Carol, what are you doing? You're stirring it in the *wrong direction!*"

In case this question ever comes up on a game show you're watching, Kool-Aid is apparently directionally-challenged and only tastes ~~good~~ like Kool-Aid if stirred in the proper direction.

I experienced the ownership of tasks again recently because my husband had to have surgery. You know how many chores around the house are "self-selected?" Okay, maybe not *selected*, maybe acquired by process of either *absence* or *elimination* when said chore comes due.

Anyway, he was not allowed to lift heavy objects or do anything strenuous, which meant that, in addition to "my" responsibilities, I took over pretty much all of his chores around the house.

Now even before going into this, I recognized that he has an emotional investment to our yard. I don't pretend to understand it, I just accept it. So I tried to respect his wishes and follow his edicts when it came to mowing the lawn.

The first thing he did was to give me a tour of our 18-hole ~~golf course~~ lawn, pointing out where the canyons were so I wouldn't fall in and be engulfed by groundhogs or tree roots.

I listened carefully and adhered to his advice on what sections to cut first. Our grass is apparently *also* directionally challenged, so I mowed following the path he recommended to get the best *nape* on the grass. I started to put the blade low enough to give ground-residing beetles a brush cut, but he vetoed this idea as bad for the blade. Then he talked me through cleaning the grass manure that clumps up on the underside of the mower carcass out with a snow brush to extend the life of the battery. I did that less often than recommended because I didn't *want* that darn battery to last longer on each round.

I think I mowed the lawn as close to his satisfaction as I could possibly get, without actually being *him*.

Then came the next task: the cat pan.

Now I should explain that, sadly, our kitty is experiencing kidney failure, which we are trying to control through diet and medication. What those measures don't control is how abundant her output is. Niagara Falls couldn't produce more clumps.

To my resourceful husband's credit, he has created a whole system in the basement for said cat pan. It includes large pan, larger "holding box" for the cat pan so the litter doesn't migrate throughout the basement, scooping scheme so litter goes in bag, which goes in plastic covered container until disposal, and entire ventilation system which safeguards against aromatherapy.

In mental preparation to work my way up to the cat pan, I began doing some of the other chores he normally handles. I emptied the dishwasher, fed and watered the cat, and began emptying the trash.

"*Wait! Wait!* Why are you emptying the trash *now*? You have to do the cat pan *first!*"

"It's okay, I'll do that next."

"*No*, you have to do that *now*, and empty it into the trash bag, because if you wait 'til trash day, it'll be too heavy!"

As I lumbered up the stairs from the basement with a kitty litter-laden trash bag after changing the pan, I had to admit he was right. I would never have suspected kitty litter could provide a full-body workout, making me wonder if Arnold Schwarzenegger got his start this way.

So I can now claim the dubious honor of being an expert in the finite art of stirring Kool-Aid, mowing the lawn and changing a cat pan.

From our current situation, I suspect I will soon become a certified expert in doing laundry in a limping washing machine, getting our home *off* the ant Conga line, and divesting our garage of a year's buildup of Amazon boxes.

Poetry

Lament for Swimsuit Shoppers, with Apologies to Lewis Carroll
2014

The time has come," the retailer said,
"To stock up many things:
Of back to school, and Halloween stuff
That make the registers ring!
And woe to those who've waited too long
To buy their summer things."

But wait a bit," the woman cried,
"Before you display all that;
I fear I still need summer clothes,
Some sunscreen and a hat!"
"Well hurry!" growled the retailer.
"My sales are getting flat!"

Laughing with the gods

"A swimming suit," the woman said,
"Is what I chiefly need...
Something fitting for the beach
Would be very good indeed.
Now that the weather's warmed up, dear,
It's urgent that I succeed."

"You'll find one here!" the retailer cried,
We still have quite a few!"
He led her toward his empty racks,
Picked over, through and through.
"The selection's fine," the retailer lied.
"Are you seeking one suit or two?"

"It was so hard for me to come!
Swimsuits make me lose my mind!"
The woman began mumbling to herself,
"Now I'm in quite a bind!
I need a suit, my old one's worn,
To wear these, I'd need to be blind!"

"It seems a shame," the retailer said,
"To play you such a trick,
You should have come *before* July 4th,
Our swimwear sells so quick!"
The woman she said nothing but
Considered giving a well-placed kick.

"I weep for you," the retailer said:
"I deeply sympathize."
But to himself he chortled,
He'd sold almost all suits in her size!
To be this low on summer stock
Was a most wonderful surprise!

"O madam," said the retailer,
"I've had such pleasant fun!
Will you be shopping here again?'
But answer came there none—
And this was scarcely odd, because
She'd turned on her heels and run.

*Inspired by "The Walrus and the Carpenter,"
with apologies to Lewis Carroll*

Valentine's Art
2019

This box is filled with Valentines.
They remind me of your smile,
As you worked with crayon, and ribbon, and lace,
Humming quietly all the while.

As I shuffle through the years of cards,
Sweet memories come unraveled,
Spooling loving thoughts around me—
My daughters, how very far you've traveled.

Those barely glued-on images,
And words scribbled in a scrawl,
Those imaginary characters,
All drawn when you were small.

Laughing with the gods

Although no longer made by hand,
Your cards still touch my heart.
Embroidered with such loving words,
All the sweeter now that we're miles apart.

Prime Day Lament
2019

Prime Day, oh Prime Day,*
I've been caught in your spell.
The credit card's maxed out,
by "treasures" priced to sell.

Did I really need that 8-man tent?
I'm not too fond of bugs.
Or that Swiss Army steak knife set?
Or faux fur matching sheepskin rugs?

Did my husband need that gaming headset
To block out household noise?
Or was it bought to mute me out,
When I complain about his "toys?"

Laughing with the gods

Did my daughters need those shredded jeans?
Theirs will be hole-y in just a while.
And woe to all those "trending deals"
That falsely claim to be in style.

As I watched the clock count swiftly down,
My panic did increase.
The race was on to get my stuff,
Before Prime Day sales would cease!

But did we need one more device
Or one more screen to view?
Is there anything we sorely lack,
Or of which we have too few?

And now that "parade of epic deals"
Has cost me near and dear.
But rest assure, it'll all be paid off
Before Black Friday deals appear!

*Prime Day is positioned by Amazon as a "two-day parade' and is an annual event with deals, product launches, and more, for Prime members.

Dieter's Dilemma
2019

As I step on the scale and the needle keeps spinning,
I'd not mind that number, if t'was the lottery I was winning!

Eat beans and eat salad, but don't dare eat rice.
You could eat pasta last year, but this year think twice.

Meat was out, now meat's in. What foods should I choose?
A full-on carb diet? Or the carb-less plate blues?

I march on the treadmill 'til I've worn out my sneaks,
"Go faster, climb higher, walk more" are my tweaks.

No dairy, no coffee? What? Give up my wine?
More fat in my diet? Well, that might be fine.

Laughing with the gods

No snacks after dinner? I'll need iron constitution.
If only some game plan would provide a solution!

One closet for thinness, for medium, and for not.
Most clothes out of style, per the retailers' plot.

One pound up, two pounds down, next week the reverse.
This dieting dilemma is simply a curse.

Eat this, don't eat that, why there seems nothing at all,
That's okay to eat, unless granularly small.

We've put men on the moon and invented AI.
There are self-driving cars and tools that can spy.

In all of these centuries humans have lived on this earth,
You'd think there'd be sure help to reduce excess girth!

Sweet Memories of Winter 2020

The winter holds sweet memories
From when I was a child,
Of wobbly skates on frozen lakes,
And winter storms so wild...

That school would close, so we could play
All day out in the snow,
Making snow forts, angels and snowmen...
It never seemed too cold.

Flying down hills on toboggans
Gave our family such a thrill,
The deeper the snow, the faster the run,
Then hot cocoa to warm the chill.

Laughing with the gods

There was such delight in winter walks,
With its crisp snow crunching sound,
And deer tracks by the frozen ponds
Always managed to astound.

We never worried about the cold,
Or icy sidewalks beneath our feet,
Jack Frost's crystal paintings on window glass
Created magic, oh so sweet.

There was no thought of heating bills,
Of shoveling walks, or driving in the snow.
No concern for "What if we get stuck?"
Or arriving on time when driving oh so slow.

With spring just around the corner,
I think I must confess...
I truly prefer sweet memories
To the reality of winter's icy mess.

Barely Two Weeks 'Til…
2022

Barely two weeks 'til Christmas and all through our house,
Decorations are missing, misplaced by some louse.
The stockings are hung by the chimney with care,
But the mantle, the window and table are bare.

No fruit cakes, no cookies, no smell of baked goods,
No candles are burning of evergreen woods.
The presents are stuffed in a closet somewhere,
In the hopes that the family will all wrap their share.

The menu's been planned, but the food's to be bought,
And the wine to match dinner is still to be sought.
The cards have been pulled out, but they sit on a shelf.
Santa better get hiring, to replace one slacker elf!

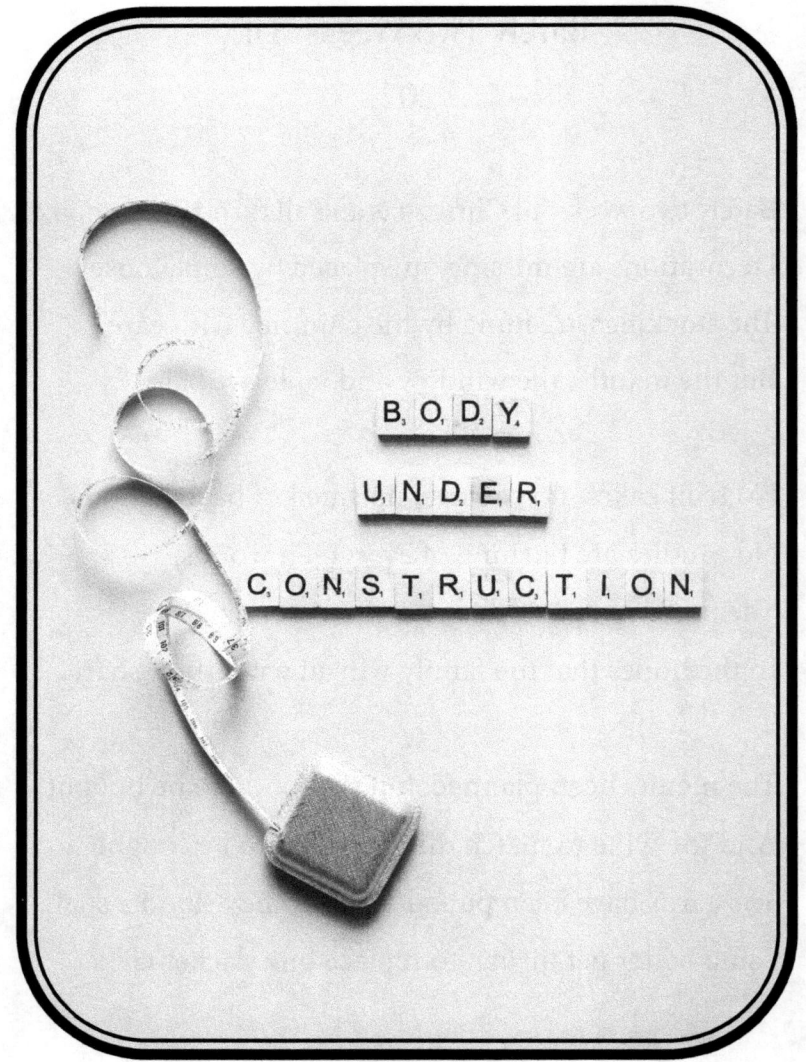

Weight Loss Blues
2023

I applaud all who work to lose weight,
This endeavor is bound to frustrate.
If there just was one key, all thin, we would be,
We could eat anything on our plate!

When you're finally determined to diet,
Each plan, app and book begs you try it.
The choices abound, some prices astound,
Kooky tips you will find are a riot.

Should you go keto or fasting or plant-based?
Your trust in one type might be misplaced!
So you try two or three, the better to see
If one program will work with more haste.

Laughing with the gods

Now you're faced with nutrition confusion!
What foods should be marked as "exclusion?"
Can you eat this or that, without gaining fat?
Might weight loss just be all an illusion?

Quite often you despair and you fail,
Each small hiccup will cause you to rail.
Hey, don't curse your sad fate, trust one trick to feel great,
Tomorrow, just don't step on the scale!

Thanksgiving Blessing
2023

May we always find light
Amidst darkness and turmoil.

May our leaders find the wisdom to resolve conflicts
And bring about peace in the world.

May we open our hearts to strangers
To discover we can be friends.

May there always be an abundance
Of food on our tables and love in our lives.

May we never give in to despair, but always express
gratitude, and seek joy, love, and hope.

Helping you skate through life with a smile

Ode to Groundhog Day
2024

Tomorrow's a strange day when many rely,
on advice from a groundhog for how long snow will fly.

Since the late 1800s guests have gathered around,
for a forecast from Phil, who ascends from the ground.

If he spots his shadow, we've a long, cold duration,
of gloves, shovels and snow boots, plus winter's frustration.

In Phil's decades of forecasts, the odds aren't too great,
that spring will come early and snow will abate.

In 12 decades of time using Phil's prognostication,
only 19 occasions were true cause for elation.

There's still reason for hope, with this plan I'll describe,
spring might just come early, if we give Phil a bribe.

Reflections & Inspiration

Au Revoir New York

2005

I am leaving New York after living here since 1983. My husband and I are moving to Western New York with our young daughters. Some friends question our sanity. Others envy our freedom. Most wonder how I'll handle the separation from a city that's been my lifeblood.

I recall the first party I attended here. It was a business event aboard the ship, Peking, anchored in the South Street Seaport. Strains of Jazz sizzled on the breeze, you could hear the rustle of people meeting as they ate and drank their way through a sea of acquaintances, and the luminescence of Manhattan at night hung like a canopy overhead.

I thought, "*This* is what I came to New York for."

And just like that, I was in love.

Now, more than twenty years later, I'm heading back to the area in which I grew up, armed with the skills, friends, contacts and experience I'd never have had if I'd stayed there. Hopefully, that will make all the difference.

Oh, but I will miss New York! Already, I feel a sense of loss and mourning for friends and the city we are leaving behind. The last weeks here are teeming with farewell gatherings and promises to keep in touch. When we do reconnect with these friends, we'll hopefully pick up where we left off. The same can't be said about New York—cities change far more quickly than people

As we arrange for movers, mail forwarding, electrical, phone and internet service—all the mundane activities that litter life's moves—I ponder how one says goodbye to a city.

Strangely, I faced this same question some 25 years ago when I moved back to Rochester, NY from the City of Lights. After a mere one year of living abroad, I found it difficult to leave, because Paris is not simply a city—it infuses the soul. Hemingway said, "If you are lucky enough to have lived in Paris as a young man, then wherever you go for the rest of your life, it stays with you, for Paris is a movable feast."

Hemingway was only half right. That sentiment applies to women as well.

Preparing to leave Paris twenty-five years ago, I found myself revisiting the places that had enchanted me while there. Preparing to leave New York, I feel the same need to make pilgrimages.

Just before leaving, I make one final trip into Manhattan. Allowing extra time between meetings, I visit places I'd missed before. Some favorites…Broadway, Central Park, Lincoln Center, East Sixth Street, The Village…we'll visit on our returns to New York. But the true jewels of this city are its gem-sized parks, unique shops and secret rendezvous locations, significant only to the individuals who discover them and make them their own.

My first stop is Bryant Park. Its ivy beds, bistro chairs and grassy lawn always felt like Paris—my Luxembourg Gardens in New York. Since my first discovery of the park, an ivy-covered café has been added, as well as a carousel for children, recalling the gaiety of the puppet theaters in the *Jardins du Luxembourg*. Missing are the *crèpes* and *glâces* stands dotting the park's periphery.

Fittingly, as I cross the flagstones toward the twirling carousel, two women behind me converse in French. I sit for a while watching laughing children ride the merry-go-round, but as rain begins to fall, I head to Lord & Taylor for my "95 scent tour" of the perfume, makeup and jewelry counters. The fragrance I associate with Lord & Taylor will forever conjure department store magic as surely as the smell of baking cookies takes me back to my grandmother's kitchen.

Next, it is time to head downtown for lunch at Les Halles, a wonderfully-French restaurant discovered while attending Baruch College. As I meander down Fifth Avenue, again I detect the lilting cadence of French. In front, two men converse in Hebrew. The flower-vendor at the deli shouts in Korean to someone inside. On another corner, I hear the rolling rhythm of Spanish. Surrounding me is a cornucopia of languages that takes me back to my first encounter with Paris and its multi-cultural ambiance.

I flourished in Paris. That city, with its medley of cuisines, languages, cultures and influences became a springboard encouraging—no—propelling me to move to New York in pursuit of new experiences. Here, I've reveled in the feast of the senses that is New York.

But now, I'm leaving. My husband and I make this choice —he with seemingly little reservation, I with much ambivalence—to slow our world so that we can enrich our daughters' childhoods by spending more time with them and to expose them to experiences the city can't offer. It feels like the right move—at least, for now.

When I moved here many years ago, my best friend Patrick, who had arrived before me to study acting said, "Living in New York is a love-hate relationship."

Mostly, I've loved it.

P.S. Sadly, as I edit this book, a number of my favorite haunts have disappeared, some falling victim to economics, others to the pandemic.

Lord & Taylor, the oldest-surviving department store chain in the United States closed its doors in 2021.

One location of Les Halles, known for its famous Executive Chef, Anthony Bourdain, closed in March 2016, and the second in 2017.

Memories of Adoption Eve
2011

Eleven years ago next Monday, we became a family. We celebrate the birth of our family much in the way others celebrate birthdays, and we call it "Family Day." Generally, we choose something special to do together on this day. When we lived in New York, we often went to Rye Playland.

Here in Rochester, we've gone to the National Museum of Play, Seabreeze Amusement Park and the Seneca Park Zoo. Last year, we spent the day running between rain drops collecting sea shells with our friends Annette and Ted, on the beach in Naples, Florida...a Family Day we'll all always treasure.

To commemorate the day, I thought I'd take you with me to the night before our twin daughters came into our family. It amazes me that it feels like only yesterday.

We had arrived in Guangzhou, China and were staying in the beautiful Five-star White Swan Hotel, a very different experience from the hotel we were at in Beijing where stingy, faulty air conditioning didn't insulate us against the 100° temperatures outside, and left a spreading puddle on the rug that we stepped in each time we entered or left the room.

Laughing with the gods

At the White Swan Hotel, there was always a young woman stationed on each floor to guide you to your room each time you stepped off the elevator in the hotel, which was configured in an 'H.' A stream flowed through the middle of the hotel lobby cascading from a three-story waterfall, caged, exotic birds serenaded the lounge area, and the breakfast buffet was fit for Kublai Khan.

We had arrived from Beijing that day, still a little jet lagged. We'd done a bit of sightseeing, so I should have been tired. Instead of tumbling asleep to dream of our adoptions taking place the next morning, I lay awake worrying far into the night, long after my husband snored softly from the adjacent twin bed, since even in a five star hotel, twin beds were the norm.

Was I worrying about the health of my daughters or about how long it would take for them to bond with us? Or concerned about the leap of faith we'd taken, adopting twins that had probably been premature? Was I apprehensive that they'd only heard Chinese for the first nine months of their lives or that we would look and probably smell so different, we'd seem like aliens to them?

No...I worried that I wouldn't be a good enough mother.

I worried that I was too selfish, too set in my ways...that I'd be reluctant to give up the many things I'd enjoyed doing as a single woman and then as a couple—the dancing and travel, shopping, movies and plays, friends and adventures.

I lay there, silent tears streaming as I envisioned the "me" I knew slipping away, drowning in diapers and bottles, nursery rhymes and strained peas, nursery school and PTA. I worried that my career would suffer and that I'd be seen as less capable. I worried that I, as I knew myself, would disappear...dissolving into my new identity as "mother of twins."

At last my fears were absorbed into the night, I fell asleep and the gritty-eyed dawn arrived. Our group of four families, filled with anticipation, boarded a bus and headed off to a governmental building to meet our long-awaited children. And in that one day, all of my fears came true, at the same time as they never materialized at all.

How do I explain it?

For a time, I did become engulfed in feedings, ear aches, diaper changes, nursery rhymes and alphabets. But the odd thing is, they enriched rather than eroded who I was... who I've become. Did my career change? Yes, but not because of my daughters, but by economic circumstances and choices I've made, both good and bad. Yes, there were times when I've wished I could put my husband and daughters in bell jars set high on shelves where they'd be safe and time wouldn't pass so that I could go off and be "my old self."

There are still days when I think that if I have to do one more load of laundry, prepare one more meal, make one more grocery shopping trip, I'll turn in my badge.

I've since discovered that's what "girlfriend getaways" are for...a chance to renew and reinvigorate. The most important thing I've realized is you don't have to love every part of the job to be a good parent. And you don't have to let go of who you are.... The parts of yourself you treasure most can be shared with your child, enriching and blossoming in both of your lives.

Cycles of Life: Outgrowing Dolly
2012

You know how artists go through periods in their career? Now, it seems, I have entered the Blue Cow period of my life.

I was on a walk this morning with our puppy Mia when I discovered that her beloved Blue Cow—the toy she insists on bringing with her on every jaunt—had fallen from my pocket. Her stuffed toy gets stowed there when she drops it the minute there's a squirrel sighting. She usually wants it again once we're on our way home.

This morning, we retraced our steps to find Blue Cow. When Mia saw it lying beside the path, she ran to retrieve it. She walked the remaining five blocks home with it clutched in her mouth, no longer trusting her treasure to my care.

It reminded me of the many times we retraced steps to find a little stuffed doll that has been my daughters' most cherished possession since my husband and I gave it to her on her first birthday.

Dolly, who was never christened with a more sophisticated name, has been a constant in our lives for the past 11 years. She has been cuddled, dropped, photographed, lost and shipped back, washed, dried and re-sewn any number of times. She has been on play dates, sleepovers, car and camping trips, stroller, airplane, and boat rides. She's one well-traveled toy.

We're now on our third iteration of Dolly, the first two having been so well-loved, that I tried to replace them with new Dolly Number Three. This last one turned out to be an imposter. She didn't "feel the same" as the prior two whose velveteen outfits have been worn threadbare by love.

In the beginning, Dolly was a constant companion, never leaving my daughter's side except for nursery school. Eventually, Dolly transformed into a nighttime-only companion. Until recently, Dolly slept under my daughter's chin, to be caressed, mushed and fondled throughout the night, even as my daughter slept soundly. My husband often teased—never in a critical way—about having to pack Dolly off to college with our daughter.

Lately, I've seen Dolly and her almost-identical sisters relegated to the foot of my daughter's bed, anchored in place only by the foot board. Each of these steps attests to my little girl's ever-increasing self-confidence. She no longer needs the reassurance Dolly once gave her.

As a parent, I am so proud of how far she has come…with her growing courage, burgeoning creativity, ripening sense of humor and blossoming personality that only comes with maturation. She's growing up…growing independent.… I wouldn't have it any other way.

Aaah, Cycles of Life.… So now, it appears, I have entered my Blue Cow period. It doesn't mean I won't still miss those sweet and poignant Dolly Years.

Random Acts of Kindness: Nothing and Everything
January 1, 2012

Have you ever had someone do something for you that meant everything to you...an unexpected kindness that touched you deeply, but that they probably chalked up as something they do, simply because of who they are?

I've experienced many examples of thoughtfulness, but several come to mind from both the distant past and a recent occurrence.

Eleven years ago, when my husband and I returned from China with our adopted twin daughters and he had to return to work, both of our daughters were ill with ear infections that the medications didn't touch. After one daughter vomited all over the three of us and a pile of clean laundry, I called Lorna, a neighbor, for advice. She volunteered to accompany me—a novice mother—to the pediatrician with my twin daughters. As if that weren't enough, she mentioned it to another neighbor who showed up at my door that evening with homemade spaghetti and meat sauce, Italian bread, salad and dessert. I almost wept, I was so touched.

Although I thanked them—I probably wrote them notes—I don't think they could ever realize what their kindness meant to me that day when I was exhausted, frazzled, insecure in my new role as mother of twins, and ill myself, as it turned out.

More recently, when I returned after a meeting to my new car that was stationed in a hotel parking lot, my passenger side window had been smashed in for the GPS that I had neglected to hide. Although there was really no harm—other than having to drive home in 40° weather with a wind tunnel running through the car—I experienced a distressing sense of violation. My friend Deb came to my rescue. Not only did she wait with me while I called the police, she treated me to dinner at the hotel while I contacted the insurance company.

If you asked any of these women about their actions, I'm sure they'd dismiss their kindness saying, "Oh, it was *nothing*." But to me, at that moment, it meant *everything*.

To you, a random act of kindness may be no more than something you'd do for any friend, or perhaps even a stranger. To them, it may mean the world.

As you enter the new year, I invite you to take a moment to think about what random acts of kindness you've been shown that meant everything to you, and to pay it forward when you have the opportunity. Your actions could mean everything to that person whose life you touch.

Helping you skate through life with a smile

Laughing with the Gods
2012

Have you ever met a person who, no matter what happens that would put others out of sorts, always seem to find humor and the bright side to everything?

My friend Elaine was sharing how, when she was driving home the other night, she could suddenly no longer see stoplights, streetlights or even be sure where she was on the road. It was as if someone had flicked off a light switch. Fortunately, her husband was in the car and he took over driving, although this was not an ideal situation either. He'd had his shoulder surgery earlier in the summer and he had to navigate home like a one-armed bandit. Elaine had experienced some vision problems earlier in the summer that seemed to be on the mend, but this incident indicates otherwise. Amazingly, as she told me the story over the phone, she was able to laugh and crack jokes about a situation that I know terrifies her.

Then there's my sister. When trying to avoid a child who cut across her path on snow skis, she "climbed" a tree. In an untimely discovery, she learned that skis are not ideal for that particular sport. The paramedics were called, and as they gently manipulated her bones to determine what damage might have been done and how to transport her to the hospital, she looked up at them, and with a grin, in spite of the pain from her fractured back, made them laugh by saying, "See? I'll do almost anything to get cute guys to feel me up!"

Thankfully, she recovered from the accident, and her sense of humor never left her.

I have seen these two women react with humor to countless situations that would put most people into an emotional tailspin.

I admire and aspire to be like them...to see life as one grand adventure, riding high on the waves of whatever the gods roll out to surprise me. Imagine being able to keep your sense of humor and laugh, no matter what your fortunes are or are not, no matter what you lose, no matter how much pain you feel....

Wouldn't it be marvelous to always be able to adjust your perspective and think "this is what is, so let me live it as an adventure!" That ability would take some of the sting out of disappointments and make even the smallest pleasures greater and the great ones extraordinary!

Laughing with the gods is surely the rarest gift to have, and one to work at cultivating.

To Live One Day Over
2012

My sister and I are very close. We've laughed, cried and shared life's triumphs and tragedies as only sisters who are also best friends can. We're "Irish twins"—born just sixteen months apart—so it always surprises me when we discover we have differing memories of the same event. Even more surprising are the rare occasions when one of us doesn't recall an incident that hangs heavily in the other's memory.

Each year at Christmas, we treat ourselves to a long conversation, since we don't get together for this holiday. This year, I asked her, "If you could go back and live one day over, which day would you pick?"

Neither of us could choose just *one* day. We started sharing favorite memories, some overlapping, others not…the choral concerts and plays…Halloween costumes and ice skating on frozen ponds…swimming lessons, camping trips, tea parties, favorite pets….

In the magic of the moment, ghosts of the past danced to life, and I was sitting on Dad's lap as he read the Sunday comics to me and I was baking Christmas cookies with Mom once again.

At one point, Ellen said, "I wish I could go back and see Mom and Dad all dressed up to go out."

And there they were in the space between us, Mom young and lovely in her favorite turquoise dress and crystals, her stole wrapped around her shoulders, and Dad so handsome in his suit, wearing his favorite striped tie. For a moment, I could almost smell his aftershave—Old Spice—that he wore when going out.

The conversation was rich in treasured memories of days we'd want to relive, to cherish once again. But we each also had a "do-over" day…a day of regret hidden deep in our memory. A day we'd relive to retract the unkind or angry words that happened between us and our father before he died, suddenly and unexpectedly, when she was thirteen and I, fourteen.

The wonderful thing about sharing all of the memories, including our one "do-over" day that neither knew haunted the other, is that they helped give perspective. I know I was able to forgive myself in realizing that one hurtful sentence was but a grain of sand in a lifetime of loving Dad.

Witihout doubt, he knew we loved him.

Dedicated to my sister and best friend, Ellen.

Aging Out of the Toy Aisle

2012

My daughters turned 13 this year. Nothing reminds me of the fact that they are growing up as much as a stroll down the toy aisle during the holiday season.

This year, as I walked through the shelves lined with dolls, stuffed animals, board games, train sets, craft items and every imaginable item paraded across the television screen on Saturday morning, I realized that my daughters have finally aged out of the toy aisle. It's a shocker. A parent never sees it coming.

The first indicator is when you don't have to spend 7 hours on Christmas eve, extricating toys from plastic, cardboard and tie wraps. The next sign is when your Christmas morning stock of batteries doesn't provide year-end dividends to Duracell investors. The final giveaway is that it becomes harder and harder to make a visual impact on Christmas morning because gift size has shrunk in inverse proportion to the size of the credit card bill arriving at the end of the month. Then comes that inglorious day when you walk down the toy aisle and discover there is *not one item* there that would delight your child.

Suddenly, all the toys you meant to buy your child—the great ideas that made it on to the list, but that you couldn't find that season, the gifts they wanted but weren't in the budget, the items you thought were a passing fancy but turned out to have been an unmet heart's desire—loom like recriminating ghosts of Christmas past.

I would be lying if I didn't admit it makes me sad that I've bought the last toys for my daughters...except for maybe a few little strange stuffed animals to decorate their beds.

Thank goodness these "lasts" are always balanced with so many wonderful "firsts"...wrapping presents by themselves for the first time, their first solo baking adventure, the first gift inspired by their imagination, rather than teacher or parent intervention....

With children, for every poignant "last," a magical "first" follows.

Invisible Ties that Bind

2014

A little over a year ago, I was in a store and heard someone say my maiden name. I turned around and there was JoAnn, a friend from grade school who I hadn't seen in decades saying, "I don't know if you remember me, but...."

I'd have known her anywhere. She still had blonde hair, and like I, she was older, a bit more *zaftig* than when we used to have sleepovers at each other's house, but there was no doubt who she was.

We got together and realized our "circle" was incomplete. We scoured social media and discovered the other two friends from our circle, and we four began meeting for lunch at different restaurants in the Finger Lakes region every couple of months or so, splitting the difference between our homes.

In many ways, we picked up where we left off, oh so many years ago when we went our separate ways after high school.

At first, I experienced a deep sense of loss at there being such a gaping hole in the quilt of our shared lives. We'd missed out on each others' adventures attending college, progressing in careers, meeting boyfriends and marrying, having children or nieces and nephews and watching them grow up.... As we shared the stories of our current lives, and looked back, new layers were slowly woven and the quilt is becoming whole again.

When we meet, I've been surprised by how often at least one of our mothers makes a "guest appearance," in spite of the fact that they are, sadly, now all gone.

Each time one of us comments, "Oh, I loved your mother's *golumpki*," or "Your mother always remembered I loved her sloppy joes and made that dish whenever I came over," leads to more conversation in which we bind together additional layers of our lives beyond our early years.

Growing up, I'm not sure any of us realized the role our friends' mothers played in our own lives. I hope they somehow knew how much they meant to us, their "surrogate daughters."

These lovely women of an earlier generation were the invisible threads that helped bind the quilt of our own rich friendship.

Choose to Twinkle

2017

About a year ago, Neil DeGrasse Tyson was a guest on *CBS This Morning*. This man should be every child's teacher, because he has a way of making science fascinating.

One of the things he discussed was the James Webb Space Telescope (JWST). He shared that this telescope is so much more powerful than the Hubble Telescope, that it will be able to "see earlier in the universe than ever before."

The JWST website explains that "The longer wavelengths enable JWST to look much closer to the beginning of time and to hunt for the unobserved formation of the first galaxies, as well as to look inside dust clouds where stars and planetary systems are forming today."

I guess because I've never taken an astronomy course, I never before thought about the fact that, when we look up at the sky in the present, those stars are so many light years away that by the time their light reaches us, we are looking back in time. Some of those stars and planets may no longer even exist.

I began to think about this concept in relation to people.

When you meet an individual, you're seeing the person he or she is today. But in reality, that individual is a culmination of all that has come before…all the people he or she has ever known, all his or her past learning and experiences—good and bad—even all of the decisions and actions of his or her ancestors.

The next time you look out across a crowd of people at a festival or a concert, think about how similar it is to gazing up at the stars at night. At first observation, it's simply a sea of people, like a sea of stars. But think about how that vision holds the key to so many amazing secrets of the past!

Now, think about *yourself*. It's easy to see your past when you look in the mirror each morning. Maybe you have your father's hair or your mother's perseverance. I know I have my grandmother's body type and my grandfather's creativity. I see persistent resilience and a complexion that burns, inherited from British Isle ancestors who came over on the Mayflower.

The thing about the person you're seeing today is, tomorrow this person will be someone slightly different, molded by the experiences of today. Recognize that you have some control over what those experiences will be, what you'll do today and how you'll enrich your own life and those around you. Today, you can choose whether your light will fade a bit, or shine a bit brighter tomorrow.

I recommend you choose to twinkle.

In Our Mother's Steps

2017

Mother's Day is a wonderful time for each of us to reflect on our own past and think about the women from whom we inherit aspects of who we are, and who we turned out to be.

My mom has been gone 15 years now, and while she and I had a fairly contentious relationship, I loved her, and there are many skills and traits she gave me for which I am thankful.

Mom didn't graduate from high school—she went back years later to get her GED, for which I was always proud of her—yet she was one of the most talented and creative women I knew.

She grew up in the shadow of the depression to which her parents lost the family home. As a result, she gained a resourcefulness that served her well her entire life, and that she passed on to her children.

When my sister and I were little, she earned extra money by sewing dance costumes for some of the girls in our neighborhood who took ballet. As I watched her carefully sewing the delicate beads onto the intricate costumes, I desperately wanted to dance, which finances and distance from the dance school made impossible. I promised myself I would learn both to sew and to dance when I was old enough. That Christmas, she asked what I wanted as a gift, and I revealed my wish.

I could barely breathe when I opened the box and found my heart's desire—a red ballerina costume, complete with little red hat, made by my mother's loving hands.

And of course, there are hundreds of other fond memories…of making ornaments and cookies for multiple holidays, of camping trips and watching fireworks, of concerts when I knew she and my father were proudly watching from the audience.

There are also the many questions I wish I had asked her… about her childhood…about our relatives and ancestors… about being a parent and how she managed life, especially after my father passed away.

On this coming Mother's Day, if your mother is alive, I invite you to pick one memory or one trait and share with her how she influenced you to walk in her steps. If she is no longer with you, why not pick one of those favorite memories and share it with friends or family so her legacy of love ripples on.

Sedona Mother

2017

Seventeen years ago this week, I lay awake in a hotel halfway around the world, staring at the ceiling long into the night. On that night, I wondered, with anxiety, how I was going to rearrange my life to become a good mother to the adoptive twin daughters I would be entrusted with the next morning.

I wanted to become a mother. That was not the issue. I had waited through not wanting children to desiring them deeply, but being with the wrong man. I had waited through breaking up with that man, dating, and finding the right one who wanted me, marriage, and children. I had waited through trying to conceive, fertility treatments and being told my eggs were "too old." I had waited through 20 months of paperwork, expecting word "any day," further delays, then receiving the joyful news of twins. The two-month wait to travel had finally elapsed, and there I was in China, filled with trepidation about my new role as mother.

Somehow, I stepped up to and into the role of being the mother I'd hoped to be. I believe I excelled at it, *most* of the time.

That is really the best we can hope for, since the role of parenting does not come with an instruction manual.

This week, seventeen years later, I find myself staring at another ceiling in a hotel in Arizona. This time, my husband snores softly at my side, and my twin daughters sleep peacefully in a queen size bed across the room. We planned this vacation to Sedona, recognizing that it might be our last as a family, at least for a while, as our daughters set off on their own for college, internships, boyfriends and first jobs.

Again, I find myself wondering how I will rearrange my life to accommodate my daughters *not* being a significant presence in each day. While I never gave up who I was during the past 17 years, my career and hobbies ebbed and flowed around parenting, and into a life that better accommodated motherhood.

Like the wind and water that slowly carved and shaped the beautiful red rock landscape that is Sedona, motherhood has worn away rough corners, unearthed vulnerabilities, and revealed an inner wellspring of emotion unknown in me before.

How will I weather these new changes?

Father's Day Tribute

2017

Some of my fondest memories of my father revolve around reading.

Every Sunday morning when I was a little girl, he gathered me into his lap and read whichever of the comic strips I pointed to. My father worked out of town a lot and was often home only on weekends, so these stolen moments meant the world to me.

On the nights that he *was* home, he would read to my younger sister and me from our book *The Bedtime Book of 365 Stories*. Once we outgrew the book, our younger brother had grown into the magic of these nightly tales. This book consisted of short stories and poems, amusingly illustrated by Richard Scary, that could be read in under five minutes. An amusing story about a lion visiting New York City fell on my birthday, and a cute poem about kittens that my sister can still recite fell on hers.

In the evening after dinner, Dad always reclined in his blue rocking chair reading a detective novel or a western. It was reassuring to see him sitting there with his book. It meant life was as it should be.

I'm sure my relationship with reading, and even writing, was influenced by the relationship I had with books as a result of my Father. I decided I wanted to be a writer early on. By sixth grade I was already crafting short stories. During my pre-teen and teenage years, I used my allowance to buy books that weren't available at the library.

It was rare that I had less than three books going at once.

Years later, when we adopted our daughters, I went on eBay and found a copy of *The Bedtime Book of 365 Stories* to share with my little ones. For my hard-to-buy-for brother's next birthday, I returned to eBay and found a second copy of this out-of-print book to give him to read to his young children.

As he opened the package, tears welled in his eyes. I knew that, in that moment, my brother was five again, and Dad was sitting next to him on the bed reading to him.

Of all the gifts he's ever received, I bet he would count that gift as among his favorites, because of the memories that flooded back as he turned each page and took on the role with his children that our beloved father had cherished.

Reminiscence of the Dog Days of Summer 2018

When I was a kid, my family lived far out in the country… or at least it seemed that way. I remember those country summers with great fondness, and probably more than a bit of time-induced nostalgia.

As summer neared its close, I and my beloved younger sister-sidekick awaited with mixed hope, dread, and anticipation those manila envelopes that would reveal the name of our teachers for the coming year. Meanwhile, she and I spent our days searching for kittens in our neighbors' hay barn, picking wildflowers that grew by the side of the road, and roving fragrant, alfalfa-laden fields in search of grasshoppers to cup gently in our hands, so we could watch them launch to freedom, from our palms.

In summer, it was almost as if there were two different worlds—one for adults, who unbuttoned shirt fronts and lifted hair from the napes of their necks, their voices lazily punctuating the hum of fans. In our world, summer flowed more languidly, for weather and temperature had little consequence.

To us, each lovely, hot, sunny, summer day made the cicadas sing and gave us reason to wade all the deeper into the cool, sun-dappled water of our neighbor's creek, in search of polliwogs and minnows. Our pup Patty—named for the Saint on whose March 17th date she was rescued from the pound—often splashed alongside, sending creek critters scurrying, and thwarting our attempts to bring home a surprise specimen to our mother, from whom we inherited our love of animals.

I realize those summers of my youth are from another moment in time, deliciously preserved in memory.

As the end of summer hastens, I invite you to think about, and savor those smells, sights, sounds and memories you cherished during an earlier time. Retrace one of those moments with someone you love by eating s'mores, collecting shells on a beach, catching fireflies, creating chalk designs on the sidewalk, playing a game of softball, or whatever activity allows you to recapture the joy of childhood's dog days of summer.

Helping you skate through life with a smile

Symphony of the Season
2017

My friend Dave Sluberski owns West Rush Media, LLC and is Senior Lecturer at RIT's School of Film and Animation, where he specializes in sound design and technology. When discussing sound design for documentaries, he often talks about capturing at least a half hour of ambient noise from your surroundings for the film's environment to give the sound authenticity. He points out that environmental sounds change on an almost-weekly basis, year-round.

To me, it seems that is never more true than in late summer and early autumn.

Woven together in a rich tapestry are the sounds of the cicadas and tree crickets, the buzzing honey bee dipping into purple asters, the whir of lawn mowers punctuated by the occasional dog barking. Add in the coo of mourning doves and the chatter of squirrels excited by the abundance of nuts that have dropped with tiny thuds.

If you could listen a little deeper, you might hear the jolting belch of a tractor coming to life, and the rickety rattle of a hay-strewn flatbed preparing to take jolly, laughing apple and pumpkin pickers into the fields on their missions of harvest.

Listen yet a little deeper and you'll no doubt hear bows being rosined and orchestras tuning for season débuts… sewing machines whirring, paint lapping at flats, and the echo of lines being practiced to empty houses as theaters yawn to life after dormant summers.

Listen even harder, and you might hear the strains of Tchaikovsky's Nutcracker Suite, as ballet shoes shush across floorboards…or tiny lilting voices reciting Dickens as auditions launch for end-of-year festivities.

Tie all these sounds up with the brilliant and sparkling gold, crimson, burnt orange and forest green ribbons of autumn's colors, and you have the makings of a magnificent symphony of autumn's sound and sight!

Thanksgiving, Family and Chocolates
2017

A number of years ago, I reconnected with my dad's side of the family. Our family had lost touch with them after he passed away when my siblings and I were young.

During our reunion weekend, I was speaking with my cousin Joan, who was born less than two weeks after me. She and I had always laughed about the fact that, had she been born first, she would have been given my name (and who knows what I'd have been named). At one point, she asked, "So what have you been up to the last 30 years?"

Thirty years? How could it have been that long? How could we, who were once as close as sisters, have let life get in the way of staying in touch?

Despite the great lapse in years since we'd seen each other, we fell into easy conversation, and we were able to pick up where we left off. Although we'll probably never be able to fill in the blanks of all that lost time, we have stayed in touch via Facebook, regardless of living half a country away. I am grateful to have reconnected with that side of my family.

Tomorrow is Thanksgiving, a holiday I associate with family more than any other holiday. I usually spend it with family, and friends who *should* be family.

I often think of Family as a box of chocolates. Most of the time, you love them to pieces. Sometimes, a little goes a long way. And even the ones that are a little nutty sweeten your life.

So this week on Thursday, I will be giving thanks for Family. I will give thanks for my wonderful husband and two amazing daughters. I will give thanks for friends who are like family and family who are friends. And I will give thanks for treasures lost, but found…those family and friends with whom I've been reunited.

What will you give thanks for?

Finding Your Next Passion
2017

Have you ever taken up a new project or started taking a class in something, and been discouraged by well-meaning friends and family that deliver pessimism on a platter? It has happened to me enough times that I'm selective about with whom I share new initiatives. I now tell only people who have a track record of being supportive and encouraging.

No matter what age we are, it's important to pursue new learning and try different things. It's also essential to accept that, initially, we won't be perfect. Failures are the hurdles we need in order to cross to the finish line. They're the learning landmarks that make us run faster and jump higher.

When I think about the importance of trying new things, I recall an incident from high school. A friend from class started coming to the music room and hanging out with those of us in chorus, despite the fact that he had never sung before.

One day, our music teacher, said, "Darwin, why don't you come over and join us in singing this piece?"

He did so reluctantly.

With the first note, out of his mouth came the most beautiful operatic baritone voice imaginable. I am not sure who was more surprised...our instructor, those of us who had never heard him sing before, or Darwin.

Mrs. Corell, who was a most inspiring instructor, immediately took him under her wing and began training him. Darwin went on to study music in college, and then to have a successful career as a church music director and religious cantor.

I've often thought, "Imagine if he hadn't been willing to try singing. Imagine if our instructor hadn't been so encouraging and supportive. He may never have found his passion."

Although this is a story about a young man finding his passion, there are many amazing stories of seasoned individuals trying new things and finding their passion as well as success, at every age. In fact, studies have shown that many artists hit their most creative spell once family has left the roost.

Whenever you think about trying something new, don't allow yourself to think "I might not be good at this," or "...at my age...." or "people will think I'm crazy...." Instead, think about how rewarding it will be when you find your next passion!"

What's Your Superpower?

2018

I recently saw *Incredibles 2*. This is the fun sequel to the animated film written and directed by Brad Bird 14 years ago, about a family with superpowers, fighting to save the world.

It got me thinking about superpowers. I realized most people possess these heightened abilities, whether or not they recognize it…perhaps not the ability to move at the speed of light or walk through walls…but unique, personal abilities they wield in their own way.

Last weekend, when I met up for lunch with three friends from grade school (we reconnected through Facebook), I think I surprised them when I asked each about her superpower. After a good laugh, and almost without hesitation, each quickly responded. Sue said, "resilience," Donna replied "my ability to empathize with others," and JoAnn noted, "The ability to make the best of everything, and laugh at whatever life throws my way."

I then asked my sister Ellen, who shared the story of telling someone she was "Never a mother, always a mom." Ellen never had children, yet she has a deep reservoir of love that she shares without reserve, and that gives her the strength to be there when others need her most, just like a mom always is.

As for my husband, years ago I recall his telling me that he felt he wasn't a "good enough" dad for our twin daughters.

"I don't know what to do with them. I just don't have your ability to connect and play with them," he worried.

Yet he found his own path, infusing his humor into parenting, and introducing our daughters to activities and events I never would have. I'm not even sure he'd see this as one of his many superpowers, but I know and appreciate that it is.

As for me, I've long considered my writing and photography to be two of my superpowers. I feel I've succeeded if I can inspire and entertain, or capture the essence of someone in a candid moment, that not only gives me pleasure, but also gives back to others.

So what's your superpower? Once you identify it, I dare you to ask your friends to share theirs! I guarantee it'll be an interesting conversation, and you might just be surprised at what you discover!

Of Sand, Snowflakes, and Humans....
2019

I recently read a fascinating article about Dr. Gary Greenberg, a biomedical researcher who started his career as a photographer and filmmaker, and who invented the high-definition 3D microscope. He has been micro-photographing sand particles at a magnification of 300 times their actual size.

It turns out that these tiny granular bits are composed of remnants of tropical sea organisms. Depending on where the sand comes from, the grains vary greatly from location to location. Their composition and appearance are affected by the temperature, surf conditions, and marine environment in which they're found.

Although no one has yet postulated it, that I know of, Dr. Greenberg's photos suggest to me that grains of sand are as unique as snowflakes, for which scientists estimate there is only about a 1 in 1 million trillion chance that any two snowflakes are alike.

Which brings me to humans. Have you ever thought about how wonderfully and truly unique each human being is?

It's something most of us probably take for granted as we go about our daily lives.

I have twin daughters, who are adopted. We know nothing of their birth family, and out of curiosity about all our blood lines, we decided to have our DNA analyzed. When we sent the cheek swabs to Ancestry.com, our daughters' analyses came back at different times. When the second report arrived, it said, "(Name of sister) is either *you*, or an identical twin."

Their DNA is that alike.

Yet as much as they look alike, have similar interests, habits, friends, and share almost the exact same DNA structure, each is as unique and beautiful as one of those microscopic grains of sand, or a snowflake.

We all are. Our heredity, family, background, life experiences and interests make us marvelously rare and irreplaceable.

So, the next time you look in a mirror and are tempted to find fault with what you see, or to criticize yourself for not having the skills or attributes of another, instead, take a moment to celebrate how very unlike anyone else you really are! No one else who came before or comes after can enrich the world in the way you can. Across the sands of time, there will be only one YOU. How fortunate are those of us who live in the right time and place to have the delight of knowing you!

Down a Garden Path
2018

As I worked in our yard this past weekend, cleaning winter's dust off furniture to get ready for what, I hope, will turn into summer, I began writing my weekly editorial in my head. It was a humor piece about gardening, because anyone who knows me, knows I capture photos of flowers and plants, because I can't keep real ones alive. But as I wove together that gardening piece—which may become a post another time—my thoughts turned to my grandparents.

They lived in Auburn, NY, where I grew up. I loved visiting them. Besides my grandmother's generous and enveloping hugs, homemade cookies, and potato soup, I remember her for her sea of African violets flooding the shelf of their southern-facing kitchen window. The trumpet-shaped honeysuckle on that side of their house drew greedy little hummingbirds to sip at the nectar, sending shock waves of perfumed sweetness rippling across the lawn on the currents of their tiny wings...a scent that will forever evoke sweet memories of her in my mind.

Behind my grandparents' yard, was around two acres of land which stretched on for what seemed like an eternity when I was a child. There, Grandpa cultivated colossal pumpkins and squash, bulbous beets, turnips, and tomatoes in the loamy soil. As a child, I thought the tassels of his cornstalks must surely tickle the clouds, they were so tall. I recall being puzzled about the horseradish. Why grow food for horses when he had none? Was it wishful thinking?

The produce they didn't give away to family, friends and neighbors, my grandmother carefully secreted away in crystalline canning jars that would reveal their savory delights when the long days of winter were upon us. A rainbow of colored glass—tomato red, pickle green, jam purple, and pepper yellow—adorned the shelves in their basement.

Theirs was a simpler, and probably healthier life, in some ways. I often wish I had their love of, and skill for growing things to nourish the body. I guess I shall content myself with capturing nature in photos, to nourish the heart and eyes.

Of Comets, Odds and Heavenly Bodies
2019

Last Friday night, my daughter Danielle and I were talking about the comet NEOWISE, named after NASA's Near-Earth Object Wide-field Infrared Survey Explorer mission. Formed of ice and dust, and measuring around 3 miles in diameter, this comet comes close enough for us to see for a period of about one month every 6,800 years.

The odds of us being here to see it reminded Danielle of something she'd learned in high school: that the odds of a human being born *at all* are infinitesimal. Out of curiosity, I looked it up and basically, humans have about a 1 in 400 trillion chance of being born.

My friend David Ross, the husband of KidsOutAndAbout.com's Publisher Debra Ross, who is a Professor at RIT's School of Mathematical Sciences and College of Science and a brilliant mathematician, would undoubtedly be able to figure out the exact odds of someone being alive right now to see it during the month or so the comet is observable. He'd probably have to adjust for the number of cloudy nights, and probably some other factors I haven't thought of, but there's no doubt the number of zeros on those odds would be astronomical.

We're living in a time of cataclysmic upheaval and change right now, because of coronavirus and political and social turmoil. Sometimes it's very hard to focus on the positive.

But somehow, when you stand under the darkened summer night sky, sprinkled with stars that twinkle like fireflies, and you can view a comet that comes along only once every 6,800 years, it helps you focus on the bigger picture...that our heavenly bodies are lucky to be here at all, and that it's important to make our shining existence count.

While we can't all be comets, we can all be stars in someone else's universe. Whose universe will you brighten today?

They Can Never Be Taken Away

2021

My close friend Debra Ross, who is the Publisher of KidsOutAndAbout.com and BeyondtheNest.com, and I were talking about the editorial she planned to write this week on the topic of people who create obstacles vs. people who create opportunities.

She's obviously the latter. Somehow, we got on the topic of past actions and achievements.

She said something I'll never forget: "No one can ever take that away from you."

I'd never really thought about that before, at least, not in those terms.

If you think back over your lifetime of activities and achievements…and even over your failures…they have undoubtedly become part of the foundation of who you are at this very moment. They have brought you rewards and awards, joys… and sometimes sorrow…but each has brought some amount of learning and growth that can never be taken away. They are core to your very being.

If you've been wise throughout your life, most of your activities have probably enriched you, at least in a personal sense, if not monetarily. On the occasions you haven't been wise—and who hasn't had a lapse of judgement?—hopefully you'll have learned important lessons, which in the long run also enrich you.

So as Thanksgiving approaches, I challenge you to think about, and even write down five things you've achieved of which you're most proud, or activities you've undertaken that have brought you the most joy. For good measure, also include five people you're most thankful to know or have known...the individuals most responsible for shaping who you are today. Take a few minutes to really think about how they have contributed to making you the person you are today.

Then enjoy a moment of thankfulness that these people and achievements are part of you and that they can never be taken away.

For Love of the Dog-eared Book
2019

I recently signed up for an online copy of the AP style book. Within minutes, I knew I wanted the print copy instead.

Although I have been a fan of the internet since its dark ages, there's something extraordinary about printed books. If you love to read, you may share my love of leafing through pages, feeling the weight of the book in your hands and caressing its spine.

When I wander into a book store or library, there's a sense of magic. I thrill to the power and energy of the authors' creativity swirling around me, like a symphony of words that is almost palpable. It feels as if every book is whispering, "Discover me! Explore me! Read me!"

Their demand is almost tangible.

When I finish reading a wondrous book, it's so hard to choose the next. There's always the risk…perhaps even fear…that it won't be as rich or rewarding or engaging as this last I've read.

Once you've found a book you truly love, chances are, you'll add it to your library, expecting to reread it again.

It may become dog-eared, from marking favorite passages and yellow from treasuring it so long. Similar to the toy in Margery Williams' book *The Velveteen Rabbit*, the book and its characters have become "real."

Although I've experienced the precious moments of J.K. Rowling bringing our family together as we traversed the magical pages of her Harry Potter series, reading is often a solitary pursuit…unless you share the love of a book with a friend.

Some of my favorite reads were recommended by fellow book enthusiasts, individually or as a result of a book club. When you share a book with another book lover… diving into a character's nuances, chewing on the plot, turning over the significance of actions…it's like sharing a good meal with friends, but with no calories or guilt!

Never underestimate the magic of the dog-eared book!

That Kind of Mom
2019

I never expected to be the kind of mom who mourns the departure of her children every time they leave… to go back to college, to study overseas, to do summer internships out of town, to visit boyfriends over Christmas vacation….and someday, to not come home for the holidays at all, and to accept jobs far away that start their new lives elsewhere.

No one warned me that I might be so invested in them, that I would feel wrenching loss each time they depart.

That emotion always sideswipes me, and simultaneously surprises me because it's not as if I didn't maintain a rich personal and professional life of my own. I never wanted to live life *through* my daughters. And here I am with my own rich life, still feeling bereft each time they go their separate ways.

Well-meaning friends assure me, "It means you've done your job! They're spreading their wings, and becoming independent. That's what you want for them, right?"

Of course it is. I love them. I want their happiness and success. I want them to be their best selves and live the most wonderful lives possible!

That doesn't mean I don't still feel a chasm of loss each time they depart.

Sometimes I run into moms who experience the opposite end of the spectrum.

"I wish my child *would* leave home!"

When I first heard someone say that, I was astounded… until I realized that kind of mother fears her child might not reach his potential…might not lead her happiest life without leaving the cocoon of home.

Then there are those—far rarer in my book—who simply accept and rejoice with each milestone their child achieves.

Actually, we all do that…rejoice and celebrate our children's milestones and achievements. It's just that some amazing moms do it without the shadow of emotions hanging like curtains in the background.

The thing about parenting is that it doesn't come with an instruction book telling you what you might feel, what you should or shouldn't do, how to be a great Mother. It's all trial and error. And love. And sometimes…guilt.

For, no matter what kind of mother you are, you often feel you could have done better. And then, you feel that if you were a really good mother, you wouldn't be feeling this way. And you don't want your child to know how you're feeling, because you don't want them to feel bad. So you ball it up and tuck it deep inside…most of the time.

That kind of mother always wants the best for her child and does the utmost to give him or her everything possible to ensure a wonderful, fulfilling life, no matter what she's feeling inside.

No one ever warns you that, no matter what kind of mother you are, no matter the age of your child, the two of you will be tied, perpetually, by the heartstrings.

Helping you skate through life with a smile

Running Away from One Too Many
2020

Have you ever felt like running away from home? I have. Just this past weekend, by chance.

I guess I attribute it to one too many dried-on coffee cup rings staring up from the counter, one too many empty toilet paper rolls not replaced by the person who finished it, one too many loads of laundry, one too many—you get the drift.

As I sat in the parking lot on one too many trips to the supermarket, realizing this mood was a momentary malaise that many experience (especially during Rochester winters) but nonetheless, contemplating where I might go if I had an escape adventure, I thought about the time I ran away as a child.

On that particular day, when I was about seven, I'd gotten yelled at one too many times. I packed a P, B & J sandwich, put some dog food and a few dog biscuits in a bag, grabbed a jacket in case it got cold overnight, my little red cart, our dog Spunky, and headed out into the fields. I didn't go far…just to the top of the hill where there was a covered well with a leafless, scrawny, skeleton tree on which a red wing black bird sat, screaming conk-la-reeeee.

I sat there, under the yawning gray sky, my arm wrapped around Spunky for comfort, to contemplate my actions while staring at our house in the distance. I realized my family might not miss me until dinner, which was hours away. I could be in the next county by then. That wasn't really what I wanted. I wanted to know I was important enough that I'd be missed. I just wanted to be appreciated, not scolded.

In the end, Spunky and I returned home. I don't think anyone ever even knew I'd run away. It was my secret.

The difference between then and now is that, as adults, we have more tools—yes, to run away—but also to make the changes to stay. We can speak up when we feel overwhelmed and underappreciated. We have the power to infuse fun in our lives when we feel yawning grayness creep in.

We just have to remember to call on those powers and use them…and to remember that our current situation is only temporary…a momentary malaise.

Saving a Sisterhood of Starfish
2020

I've been collaborating on a project called Women and the Vote NYS (womenandthevotenys.com). A diverse group of women is doing research to create a database of suffragists buried across New York State.

My initial involvement was to help populate the database for a documentary we plan to make*. The database will help visitors find places to pay tribute to suffragists, as happened at Susan B. Anthony's grave site during the 2016 election. We plan to have filmmakers on site at the cemeteries to interview visitors. Assuming we can go forward with the film, it will undoubtedly be a fascinating dialogue, in the wake of COVID-19.

Quickly, my purpose for involvement expanded. You see, so many of the women who *should* have been heralded for helping women achieve the right to vote have been all but lost to history.

Each week, our small group sifts through online websites and documents to discover shreds of information that will lead to the occasional bio, or grave site. Often, these women are obscured by married names, burial in her husband's family plot, or their lack of financial clout.

Even when the women have made great contributions to society, the grains of their lives have been washed away by time.

We've managed to "reclaim" fascinating women from all walks of life. There have been opera singers and actors, educators and lawyers, farm and factory workers, dentists and doctors. In recent weeks, I rejoiced to "reclaim" the first woman admitted to the Bar in NYS, the educator who founded Lochland School for the disabled in Geneva, NY and the only signer of the Declaration of Sentiments who lived long enough to enjoy the fruits of her labor.

We have unearthed breathtaking accomplishments, jaw-dropping scandals, and a sisterhood forged of adversity—because getting the vote was a long, arduous, and often dangerous pursuit. Suffragists fought off police and political brutality as often as the violence born of a populist anti-suffragist sentiment.

Each time I'm able to reclaim the history and grave site of a suffragist, I feel like the starfish thrower, who, when confronted with a beach full of marooned starfish, throws them back one-by-one into the sea to live again.

Each time I find another, I think, "I saved this one," as I see my suffragist come to life in words and, occasionally, photos. They may never know of their success, but we will...now.

I am proud to share that the film, Women and the Vote, directed and produced by Linda Moroney of Low to the Ground Productions, and on which I was honored to be a Field Producer, won a NYS Emmy Award. Filmed on Election Day 2020, the documentary reflects on New York's suffrage legacy and was the direct result of this initiative. For more on the film, visit: www.pbs.org/show/women-and-vote/.

Of Verandas, Communications and Cororavirus
2020

Have you ever thought about how our outdoor space has altered to reflect the changes in our communications?

In my grandparents' days, it was common for houses to have sprawling verandas and welcoming front porches facing the streets, so home owners could catch cool breezes on warm summer days and chat with folks passing by. In that way, everyone kept up on community gossip and the news of the day. These architectural additions were not just a barrier, or even a transition between the outdoors and the interior of a house, these spaces were gathering places, protecting the privacy of the home and family, while providing hospitality.

Then, as automobiles gained more prominence, making streets noisier, and as TVs, fans and air conditioners became American staples, front porches shrank in popularity and size, eventually giving way to back decks and patios. Although I'm no architectural historian, it feels as if there's a direct correlation between the 24/7 news and social media cycles and the disappearance of space in which to engage with the broader community. In many neighborhoods—mine for example—residents know each other mostly through the dogs they walk. Front porches were to engage with everyone, back decks and patios welcome selective few.

Think about our communications for a minute. We're battered all day long by people wanting to "break down our front door." We're bombarded with emails, newsletters, newspapers and magazines, TV and radio ads, snail mail, social media, iMessenger, Facebook calls, texts, Slacks, phone calls, and now Zooms and webinars. If alterations in our exterior space reflect these changing communications, it's a wonder we haven't all built moats around our houses.

Now, that the coronavirus that has become an unwelcome visitor for what appears will be the long haul, what I wouldn't give for a good, old-fashioned, giant, wrap-around veranda, onto which I can invite friends, and the passing neighbor for long chats in person, while still socially distancing.

Architects, are you listening?

Too Much *Feng* in Your *Shui*?
2020

In an effort to improve the *feng shui* of my house, I recently decided to declutter. Wikipedia defines *Feng Shui* as a "traditional practice originating from ancient China, which claims to use energy forces to harmonize individuals with their surrounding environment."

I definitely need a little harmonizing about now, but that clutter seems to understand the laws of physics better than I do, because those bodies of clutter that were at rest around the house are mostly still in place, and not at rest curbside, ready to enhance the *feng shui* of the garbage truck.

The other issue with clutter is that it tends to derive energy from memories ensconced within. Once you disturb that energy by moving the clutter, it's as if you've awoken Mulan's entire sparring Fa family ancestors.

"What? You're going to throw out that lovely brown sweater I knitted for you 30 plus years ago?" asks Mom's hurt voice within my head.

"You're worried about a sweater?! What about that patchwork quilt she's put on the discard pile? I hand-sewed it more than 80 years ago, made from my family's most beloved and cherished shirts and dresses? How can she

Laughing with the gods

throw that out?!" asks Great Aunt Louise, seemingly as upset with Mom as with me.

Mom again, "Your quilt's got rips in the fabric. It's not even that warm anymore!"

"Your sweater's got pulls – and she never did find buttons to put on it!" fires back Great Aunt Louise, eager to have the last word.

Their voices quiet as I appease them by laying the sweater and quilt gently back in their storage chest.

Even my daughters have come under this influence. Danielle is redecorating her room. In order to paint, she decided to get rid of her collection of 547 stuffed animals. She bravely put them in bags and carted them off to donate. When she returned, her six-foot stuffed bear was in the passenger seat.

"I left him sitting on the pile, and when I looked back, he looked so sad…. I just couldn't bear to leave him. Besides, Aunt Ellen and Uncle Bobby gave him to me."

I guess some things just have too much *feng* in their *shui* to be decluttered.

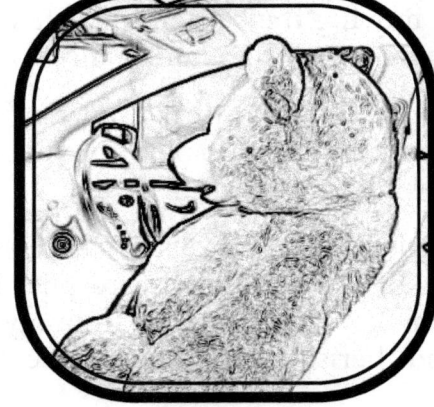

Helping you skate through life with a smile

Preserving Mother's Day Memories
May 2021

With Mother's Day right around the corner, I bet there are a lot of other women, like myself, who wish they could turn back time.

From the bell jar of my memory, where they've been exquisitely preserved, I recall many sweet Mother's Days when my daughters, husband and I were together as a family at Rochester's Lilac Festival, perusing the crafts, munching on lobster rolls or fried dough, wandering the lilac scented paths, and taking selfies in our favorite "twisted tree."

It's odd that when you become a mother, you're not told that it *is*, and it *isn't* a forever role. It can feel like forever during those times when the kids are acting up and you're at wits' end, when they're ill and you're worried sick, or when they're having school or dating problems and you feel helpless. You want it to be forever during those sweet moments when they crawl into your lap just to cuddle, or you realize their sense of humor is emerging by the way they make you laugh, or when they give you a hand-crafted piece of art just to say "I Love You."

There's the time when it feels like they need you every minute of every day...right through to the time when it feels like they no longer *need* you much at all. If you're lucky, they'll always *want* you as a friend.

No one warns you that one day the role that's existed throughout your child's entire life will suddenly shift cataclysmically, to the point where phone calls must suffice in place of hugs.

As mothers, we rejoice in their independence because it means we've done our job well, at the same time as we are saddened because it means we've been retired all too soon.

As women, we are the daughters who never understood these things when we were growing up, to notice or to have empathy for our mothers feeling the weight of our absence. And we are the mothers who understand these things all too well.

So to all of the women reading this, whether you are a mother, a daughter, or both, I wish you a Happy Mother's Day, and many, many more sweet moments to preserve in the bell jar of your memory.

The Summer of the Caterpillar Coat
2021

As a girl, I lived out in the country. I remember long, magical summers when my sister and I would run through fields chasing butterflies, roll in alfalfa, wade in the creek, and play hide and seek among tall cornstalks.

One summer when I was about six, caterpillars were abundant, and I begin collecting them. I didn't realize that I might be downsizing the butterfly population; I just knew I loved the tickly, furry, fuzzy little creatures.

Soon after I began collecting them relatives visited. My aunt asked, "Carol what are you going to do with them?"

I hadn't thought about that. I considered the question for a moment, then answered, "I'm going to make Mom a caterpillar coat!"

When she laughed and asked, "How are you going to do that?" I responded that I wasn't sure yet, but I would figure it out.

I guess I never thought about what would happen to my beloved caterpillars in the process of making a coat.

Soon my caterpillar collection became so abundant that I needed a bigger container in which to store them, so I borrowed my father's minnow bucket. I left it outside on the porch, adding leaves and milkweed pods for my caterpillars to eat. They seemed to be thriving...until the night it poured rain.

Now, if you know anything about minnow buckets, you know that, when they're filled to the brim with water, they're great for keeping small fish alive, but not so great for fluffy caterpillars.

Alas, all hundred or more of my little caterpillars had kicked the bucket .

I'm not sure how mom felt, but I was *devastated* for my fuzzy friends. Yet I was also half-relieved that the conundrum of how to create a caterpillar coat had been eliminated.

I think of that caterpillar coat story often because it's a metaphor for creativity. Often, we come up with a "caterpillar coat" idea, and people laugh, or we're stymied to find a solution on how to do it, we don't have the money to bring it about, or we simply give up on the challenge. This is not bad if it wasn't a great idea to begin with.

But the real challenge is to differentiate between the caterpillar coat and an idea that is truly innovative and world-changing. Sometimes there's a very fine line between the two, and you might not know the difference until you try it. Just think about all the naysayers who considered Thomas Edison's, Jonas Salk's, Bill Gates', and Steve Jobs' ideas "caterpillar coats" in the beginning.

Traditions Warm and Wonderful
December 2021

I put up our Nativity scene last weekend. It's a vintage manger with much-loved and slightly time-worn figurines that I inherited from my mother. You've probably seen similar versions at garage sales or antique stores.

For some reason, it never got set up last year. But since this is the 20th anniversary of my mom's passing, I wanted to set it up this year, in her honor.

As I gently unwrapped the figurines, I recall how she, my sister and I would make a pilgrimage to the local discount department store each year to pick out one or two more figurines to add to the scene...maybe a sheep or the goat, an angel, a camel, or a shepherd. I never realized at that time how the purchase of even those tiny nativity pieces undoubtedly put a strain on our family budget.

One new piece would join the stable scene, then be carefully wrapped away each year to be opened the next by two wide-eyed sisters, always intent on being the lucky one to unwrap the baby Jesus.

Laughing with the gods

The little nativity wears a history of love, having adorned a shelf or table almost every Christmas since before I was born. It is still stored in the time-stained Gerber baby food box with my mother's elegant handwriting "creche" on a peeling-off label so it could be found on the shelves amid other holiday treasures. Several figures are missing a paint chip or two and the manger is now bereft of the straw that was there in years gone by.

I've often seen other similar sets and could have easily added to the set or replaced imperfect pieces. I've chosen to keep it exactly as I inherited it. I suppose in some ways, it reflects how time has chipped away at me and worn away some of my "edges" over the years. Besides, some traditions are too precious to change.

Whatever your religion, beliefs, and practices, here's wishing you a holiday season rich in warm and wonderful memories and traditions.

Hoarding Memories
2022

It started with a search through my well-loved recipe box, looking for my raggedy Spanish Rice recipe card. Before I knew it, all of the recipe cards were strewn across the table in spectacular disarray. Scattered among them were my grandmother's sugar cookie recipe, my Aunt Jeanette's "Wacky Cake," and the recipe for "glop," a delicious, but peculiarly-named cheese dip that an ex-boyfriend's mother shared with me. There was also a multitude of recipes I didn't recognize and have probably never made.

As I sifted through them, memories of family dinners, evenings with friends, and misguided experimental dinners that often involved cinnamon drifted to mind.

These days, it's rare that I turn to a recipe book or my recipe box. I'm more likely to go online for a recipe. At other times, I rely on my own culinary creativity to innovate new recipes.

As I looked through the cards, trying to discard those I no longer use, and the ones I took in deference to the person sharing them rather than my love of the dish, I found it surprisingly hard to throw them out… especially the ones penned in the handwriting of a person no longer around.

So, I culled about a half dozen from the box, threw them out, and called it a day. I tucked the rest gently back in the box, in a slightly more organized fashion than they came out, and reverently replaced the box back on its shelf.

Now, I've never considered myself a hoarder of things, but I guess when it comes to hoarding memories, I'm guilty. Sometimes those memories have items attached, sometimes not.

Often the memories associated with food hold a very significant place in our minds. There's something about gathering with family and friends over a delicious meal, often for holidays of one sort or other, that makes those memories indelible, and the tangible items associated with them, difficult to part with. I think the originators of those recipes would be flattered.

Aging Gracefully into the True You

2021

Last week, I celebrated my birthday. It wasn't a landmark (or landmine) event, just an every year sort of birthday. But since then, I've been thinking about the subject of aging. After all, it's an inescapable fact of life, and there's a big difference between aging and growing old. I believe it's something over which we have control. I've thought a lot about my philosophies on aging, and I share them in the hopes that they offer an alternate perspective on the process of becoming an Elder:

- Don't own your maladies. Many people refer to "*my* arthritis," "*my* diabetes," or "*my* [fill in the blank]." By referring to the disorder in this way, you own it, identify with it, and claim it as yours. It becomes part of who you are. Who would want to own an illness? It's better to simply acknowledge that you have it, but not allow it to become part of who you are. By saying you *have* an illness, you are simply accepting reality. By calling it "my," you are giving it power over you and how you live and perceive your life.
- Never refer to yourself as old, no matter what age you are. You're aging. We all are. That is all. By referring to

yourself as old, that is the status with which you are identifying, and you are accepting society's perception, and even definition of age (which sadly, often has negative connotations). It erases your ability to define it for yourself. You have the power and every right to define yourself as you wish. Encourage friends and family around you to accept and follow these rules for themselves as well. That way, you'll be surrounded by a host of people who are ageless.

- Celebrate yourself! You gotten to this point, now find something you want to do to celebrate it *every day*. Find an activity you enjoy and make it part of your daily routine bringing you joy...whether it's reading, gardening, crossword puzzles, martial arts, walking, spending time with family and friend, or whatever. The best way to celebrate yourself, not just on your birthday, but every day, is just by being *YOU!*

Helping you skate through life with a smile

Out of the Darkness: Light One Candle
2022

On Sunday, (March 20, 2022) I saw a story on ABC News about a Ukrainian violinist named Vera Lytovchenko who is performing in the war-torn basement bomb shelter of her apartment building in Kharkiv for friends and neighbors seeking shelter there. The videos she posts online have gone viral.

Vera, who is a member of the Kharkiv City Opera Orchestra, dresses in performance attire, as if entertaining on the most elegant of world stages: Her audience deserves nothing less. Many have written, thanking her.

When asked why she plays, she responds of her viewers, many of whom are in Ukraine, "My video helped them to be not so alone and to feel more strength…to be able to distract for several minutes, and to not just think about war, to think about something better."

She does not plan to leave her city, despite the fact that bombs have exploded very close to where she is sheltering.

When I posted on social media about an initiative the school at which I work had undertaken to raise money and send medical supplies to help the Ukrainian people, a man named Ilya posted the comment, "Thank you so much," in Russian.

We exchanged posts, and he wrote that he knows many people in Rochester from Ukraine. I commented how hard it is to see what is happening there and to wish there was more that can be done, or to have family or friends in Ukraine and feel helpless to assist them.

His comment was priceless: "Doing a little is doing a lot. Small impacts eventually turn into big ones."

How right he is. Whatever you do to "light one candle," shining light through the darkness, as Vera does, matters. It can inspire comfort or courage. I think of the Peter, Paul and Mary song "Light One Candle," written so many years ago, that I find so relevant today:

"Light one candle for the strength we all need

To never become our own foe!

And light one candle for those who are suff'ring

Pain we learned so long ago!

Light one candle for all we believe in,

Let anger not tear us apart!

And light one candle to bind us together

With peace as the song in our heart!"

May we all be the bearer of candles.

Written in solidarity with and celebration of the courage and perseverance of the Ukranian people.

Helping you skate through life with a smile

Carpe Diem: The Future Is in Your Hands!
2022

When I worked as an executive at a trade association in New York City, the receptionist was a good friend. Joan was an elegant, lovely, mature lady who had been the wife of the conductor of the Longines Symphonette. She and her husband had hosted musical soirees in their living room while he was alive, where she sang opera for their friends. One summer day shortly after her 80th birthday, as she walked to work—yes, she was still working—a USPS truck driver didn't see her in his rearview mirror and backed into her, knocking her down. Although she recovered, she was the worse for wear.

I'm not sure whether her sight issues were already coming on, or whether the accident caused the issue but she ended up being forced to retire shortly thereafter, because of macular degeneration.

I loved visiting her when I could—she was always full of wonderful stories—but one day, I was saddened when she said, "I always expected to paint and play music when I retired, but now I can't see and I can't hear well, so I can't do any of the things I had hoped to have time to do."

I write this because a beloved family member is retiring today, due to a degenerative condition, and he has ambivalent feelings about leaving a job from which he has derived so much satisfaction as well as identity for so many years. When he and I spoke over the weekend, Joan's words came back to haunt me when he said, "I always expected to be able to do all these different things when I retired, but now...."

I share these stories today to extend a challenge: no matter what age you are, do not wait for some future moment in time to do the things you want to do. Do them *NOW!* Do them while you can still enjoy them. Do them so they infuse your soul, your life, and your time with joy.

Play that game of golf, join that choir, take up those dance lessons, travel to those distant lands you always wanted to go to. Don't wait for the house to be perfect to invite those friends in for dinner. Figure out a way to do these activities, to fit them in your budget and your time now.

Today is within your grasp, and who knows what tomorrow may bring? Carpe Diem...Seize the Day so there will be no regrets over the things you never got to or can no longer undertake that you'd always planned on doing. Your future is in your hands!

Helping you skate through life with a smile

Making Time Stand Still
2022

One of the students at the school where I work declined to have her photo taken for the yearbook. Years from now, when she opens the yearbook, there will be no record of who she is in this moment...a beautiful young lady, on the precipice of adulthood, with hot pink hair and a shy smile that lights up the room when she chooses to show it.

I wish she could have been at the event I attended this past weekend.

On the occasion of their 40th Anniversary, our friends Elaine and Hank renewed their vows in a beautiful, funny, and touching ceremony, followed by a reception.

They were surrounded by friends and family, many of whom they've known consistently for many years, and others of whom have somehow magically reappeared in their lives after periods of absence. Even six of Elaine's original eight bridesmaids were in attendance.

Before the event, Elaine foraged through her treasure trove of photos so her son and I could put together a slideshow of photos from over the years, set to music. The voices of Dan Fogelberg, The Birds, John Denver and other 70s and 80s minstrels added ambience to college and wedding photos, Halloween parties, the birth of children, pumpkin picking, and the opening of Christmas gifts.

Elaine had carefully ensured that there would be at least one photo of each person in attendance among the photo montage.

As photographer for the occasion, I stood in front, waiting to capture expressions as their friends watched the time capsule, taking them back 20...30....40 years. I was struck by the power of this simple slide show. Smiles and tears, laughter and love filled the room. It was an opportunity to experience, even relive for a moment, memories of earlier times and events, made even sweeter by the passing of time.

If my young friend could have been there, perhaps she would change her mind on having her photo taken, for she would understand how important it is to make time stand still, if even for a moment.

Helping you skate through life with a smile

Riding a Bike at Dusk
2022

I went out for a walk the other night around 8:30 pm, when it was getting toward dusk. As I walked down the sidewalk near our home, a little girl approached me on bicycle and said, "hello."

I greeted her back and complimented her on her bike riding. I sensed she was heading home.

She was probably around eight years old, and I couldn't help thinking how lucky she is to live in a neighborhood safe enough that she can ride her bike at dusk.

When I was a child, our rural neighborhood always felt safe. Summer was a time of magic, joy, and wonder. My sister and I lived outdoors until dinner. Even after dusk, we sometimes played games outdoors in the dark, with only the lightning bugs, moon, and stars as illumination. That's how safe we felt. That freedom is not commonplace today.

As parents and grandparents, we must call on our leaders to find a way to take us to safer times, where citizens can safely shop in supermarkets, and children can attend school without fear of gunshots ringing out...a place where bombs and mortar shells are not falling in distant lands disrupting the lives of families overseas, and endangering the lives of our men and women fighting for freedom.

Whether we are Democrat, Republican, or Independent, and no matter our ethnicity or spiritual inclination, we all want the same—safety for our families and friends, that we may be allowed to love and learn and enjoy leisure in peace.

Let us work together—leaders and "political adversaries," neighbors and friends—to find solutions to problems, mend grievances, and return the world to a place where children will feel safe walking through the school doors and riding their bikes at dusk.

And if we cannot *find* those leaders who can bring peace and safety to the world, may we find the courage and wisdom to *become* those leaders. Our world demands and deserves nothing less.

Written in the aftermath of the Supermarket shooting in Buffalo, NY, and the school shooting in Uvalde, TX.

Today's My Lucky Day!
2022

Have you seen the lovely, uplifting film *Mrs. Harris Goes to Paris*? In case not, it's the story of a British cleaning woman in the 1950s whose client has purchased a gorgeous Christian Dior dress. Mrs. Harris falls in love with its beauty and decides to save enough money to go to Paris to buy one for herself.

Mrs. Harris is a charming woman who manages to attract people to her with the force of her down-to-earth, genuine personality. When people encounter her, and ask how she is, she responds, "Today's my lucky day!"

They may wonder whether she considers herself lucky because she's having a terrific day, or because she just met up with *them*. What would you imagine? And who wouldn't be attracted to this type of positivity?

What is equally fascinating is that she has a sweet and persistent assertiveness, and somehow manages to get most things to go her way, whether that is having a Marquis invite her to be his guest to view Christian Dior's new collection, or serendipitously being invited to stay at one of Dior's employee's homes while she waits to be fitted for her dream creation.

Now, she *does* seem to have a fair amount of luck, but whether she actually has more than normal people is questionable. I suspect we all have a comparable amount on any given day. The difference between Mrs. Harris and most people is that she is *actively looking* for good luck, as well as signs that it may be coming her way.

Imagine waking each morning thinking, "Today's my lucky day." Consider what might be in store for you, if that was the first thing you thought as you're having your coffee or breakfast! Starting a day off that way, you probably would have more luck—maybe because you attract it to you—but more likely, because your focus has shifted to perceive the ordinary as extraordinary!

If you believe in the power of positive thinking—and I hope you do—try sprinkling a little of that attitude in your coffee or on your cereal each morning to start your day!

Mother's Day Message on Live Action Parenting 2022

Was that I you I heard muttering under your breath, saying something about not being a good mother? I thought so.

I don't know why, but I've heard a lot—too many—friends who are GREAT mothers "admit" that recently. Actually, I don't know many women who haven't mumbled that at one time or other. You're in good company.

Perhaps that thought ran through your mind because you were late taking your daughter to her dance class, or because you missed your son's karate exhibition due to a work conflict. Maybe your kids are six months overdue on their dental check-ups, or you're not home in time to help your kids with homework. Perhaps you couldn't afford that one special birthday present your son really wanted, or you lost patience with your daughter over her indecision or insolence. There are thousands of reasons we think ourselves unworthy or unfit mothers.

If you worry about these things, I'm guessing you're actually a pretty terrific parent. Maybe just a wee bit imperfect. Most parents are.

Parenting is a lot like playing video games. I know whereof I speak, since my daughters are 22, and on to the next phase of their lives. That means that as a "game playing" parent, I've "advanced" to the Zoom version of Parenting: I can look on and advise, but the remote contols to the game have been forever removed, almost overnight.

If you have kids below high school, you're probably still in the Live Action phase of playing. The thing about gaming is, it comes with no players' manual. Oh, you can find tips, tricks and hacks online and in books, but the ABCs of playing—Advisor and Advocate, Butler, Chef, Chauffeur and Cheerleader—are all learned only by the trial-and-error version of playing.

The problem with that is that the rules keep changing as you play.

I remember a video game my daughters enjoyed when they were young called *Animal Crossing*. You wandered through the game as a character (or avatar, if you prefer), without rhyme or reason, undertaking activities, without knowing why or what you were doing. When you ran into an apple tree and shook it, time after time, loads of money would come floating down. *Until* the time you shook it and bees swarmed out

That illustrates the reality of Live Action Parenting. Think about the treat you give your child that always elicits a smile…until the time you're suddenly accused of sabotaging her diet or trying to throw him off his wrestling weight.

Bottom line? You just have to accept that you'll never be perfect at Live Action Parenting. But that's okay. Try to remember that they may not always remember the loving things you do for them with their mind, but they'll always remember those things with their heart. And that's where it counts most.

What about all the goofs, mishaps, and mistakes? Oh, your kids will remember *those* things until the end of time! But one day...perhaps some 10 or 20 years down the road...those upsets will become fodder for loving laughter and happy memories.

So to all of you wonderful Moms out there, may you face your parenting "imperfections" with grace, laughter, and self-forgiveness. And may your children come to see you for the really great parent you are!

We Are All Fireflies
2022

It's too early in the season to see fireflies, but I bet you can recall a time during a past summer when you've been outdoors, gazing across your backyard or an open field, seeing the twinkling dance of the fireflies. It's magical, isn't it? They sparkle in one spot, for a moment, and then disappear into the darkness, weaving their way invisibly across time and space until they sparkle again in another location.

I ask you now to think about all of us as fireflies. There are times when we sparkle—when we're in love or doing what we love, when we're at our best, giving of ourselves to others, and when we're loving life. There can be times—when we're in the wrong job or going through hard times physically or emotionally—when we may not *be* invisible, but we *feel* that way. Even for those of us who prefer not to be in the limelight, feeling invisible—as if we don't matter—is not a welcome state.

When you're in a situation where you feel invisible, you may not always be able to completely change your circumstances, but you can find ways to shine again. Perhaps it means exploring a new hobby or taking up an activity you've always wanted to try. Maybe it entails becoming involved in volunteer work or undertaking some kindness for friends. Maybe it's an act of generosity. Occasionally, it might require work with a mental health professional to recapture your inner glow.

We also shine when we do things that encourage others to sparkle...when we help lift them out of the darkness, even if for only one smiling moment, through something we say or do. Maybe it's recognizing them for a skill or complimenting them on something they're wearing. Maybe it's cooking their favorite dish or giving them a small token to show how much they mean to us. Perhaps it's connecting deeply over a conversation. This person could be someone we love, a friend, or a complete stranger.

Fireflies don't twinkle all the time. Neither can we. But we all deserve to feel that sparkle some of the time. The darker it gets, the more important it is to find that glow.

If you've lost your sparkle, I challenge you to work at recapturing it through action. I also challenge you to go out of your way to add sparkle to someone else's day. And I guaranteed that seeing a smile on someone else's face or hearing a word of thanks from them will help ignite the glow within you.

Summer Fair Nostalgia

2022

Remember when you were a kid and you waited all summer for the firemen's carnival, or the county or state fair?

You'd jump out of the car in the long, tickly grass of a field-turned-parking lot studded with lightning bugs and make your way, as night settled, toward the giddy sounds and heady smells wafting on the breeze from the midway. Depending on your age, you might have pretended you didn't know those parents holding hands and walking annoyingly closely behind you.

You'd arrived, but where to start? The challenge was always how to make your allowance stretch across all the amusement park rides and foods you wanted to sample, always saving just enough for the spun, sugary, cotton candy confection available only once-a-year.

Those Firemen's carnivals and county fairs were a far cry from today's amusement parks, but we had no comparison, so they seemed thrilling.

At 12, I had romance envy, thinking of my crush-du-jour, that I could only *wish* I'd get stuck with at the top of the Ferris wheel, hoping to experience my first kiss. Alas, it took four more years, while volunteering at the Duchess County Fair during a summer visit with a school friend who had moved to Poughkeepsie before I got my wish. I can't hear a certain song without thinking of a handsome, dark-haired boy named Paul—also a volunteer—who was unphased by the fact that I towered over him by at least five inches. As jewel lights twinkled across the midway, my heart fluttered from cotton candy kisses bestowed before the Ferris wheel glided back to earth.

I'm sure you have your own nostalgia-laced memories of fairs and festivals from the past. Wouldn't this be a good summer to revisit them?

It Tastes Like Christmas
2022

When my daughter Danielle and her Swedish boyfriend Eric came home for the holidays last December, they brought an assortment of tasty treats from his homeland, where she now lives. One was a drink called *Julmust**, *Jul* from the Swedish language referring to Christmas, and *must* from Britain, referring to a juice that is not fermented. Introducing it to us, Eric commented that the drink "tastes like Christmas" to him.

Isn't it funny how a taste can bring back memories? For many people, fresh strawberries taste like summer. For me, it's watermelon. Potato soup takes me back to my grandmother's cozy kitchen, with African violets soaking up sunlight in the corner.

Scents do the same. If you revisit your grammar school, you just might be transported back by the smells of melted crayons, tempera paint and disinfectant. When I walked into my grammar school for the first time in many years, it smelled *exactly* the same, sending me suddenly back to 4th grade with my favorite grammar school teacher, Mrs. Graham.

If you ever sell a house, your realtor may suggest baking an apple pie or chocolate chip cookies before your prospective buyers arrive to evoke memories of home.

Music has a similar power. If music was playing the first time you were ever kissed, I guarantee you'll be transported to that moment each time you hear that song. You'll probably remember the young man's or woman's name as well.

While most of us rely heavily on our vision, the other senses play a subtle but strong role in our day-to-day life. I like to think of it as part science, part magic, but whatever the mix, why not indulge and celebrate the senses?

Light candles, indulge yourself with a bouquet of flowers once in a while, stop for a moment to take in the aroma of the grass you've just mowed, bake a cake or pie without worrying about calories, use a shower balm when you bathe. For a change in your work or home soundscape, sample different types of music, put up windchimes, or play ambient sounds while you're working or just relaxing.

Your senses will appreciate your generosity.

* *Jul*, sounds very similar to 'jewel,' with a 'y' instead of a 'j,' and "*must*," with the 'u' sounding like the 'oo' in cook.

Excuses Masquerading as Reasons

2023

Have you ever thought how often excuses masquerade as reasons?

I was in my doctor's office due to a shin and ankle injury. She asked how much exercise I get. The first thought that popped into my head was "A lot less since our dog passed away and I don't walk her anymore."

While that is true, it's also a pretty—excuse the expression—lame excuse for lack of exercise. I didn't say it aloud.

Instead, I candidly responded, "Not much right now because of the injury," reflecting on my frustration over the vacation adventure that caused the injury, forcing me to postpone the exercise plan I'd committed to on vacation. It's an annoying, but legitimate temporary reason for lack of exercise.

When she asked about adding more fiber to my diet—vegetables and grains—I responded, "They're such a pain to pack for work."

The minute that was out of my mouth, I could hear the ridiculousness of the excuse. I tried to ignore her raised eyebrow. The next day, I changed my lunch packing habits.

The thing about excuses is that they absolve accountability without true legitimacy. They somehow make you *feel* better about things you've done that you shouldn't have, or things you haven't done that you should have, even though they're not genuine reasons.

It's important to "size up" excuses that may be masquerading as reasons, especially for bigger considerations, such as savings, overall health, family relations, the achievement of desired goals, and other key life decisions and actions.

Once you examine excuses under the harsh light of rationality, you might be motivated to change. Unhealthy habits and unwise choices may actually move in a more positive direction once you examine and recognize an excuse for what it is.

If you look at excuses carefully and recognize them for what they really are, but still do nothing about them, dig a little deeper. You may discover that beneath those excuses is either something that really doesn't matter to you, or there may be an underlying fear holding you back. If it's fear, and you examine it for what it is, you may be able to let go, remove the excuse, and move on.

Fear of the Flop
2023

"I've missed more than 9000 shots in my career. I've lost almost 300 games. 26 times I've been trusted to take the game-winning shot and missed. I've failed over and over and over again in my life. And that is why I succeed."

– Michael Jordan

It's impossible to go through life without failure and mistakes, and yet many people are afraid of them.

I still have a hard time thinking about my biggest flop. It was a travel magazine franchise I bought many years ago. It was just beginning to take root when the recession of 2008 hit. In a recession, the first thing companies cut back on is advertising. My magazine died, taking with it my entire investment, my self-esteem and my dream.

I'd poured over two years, spending thousands of hours and dollars, into it. I was devastated, and it took me a very long time to get over it and recover from the depression that crashed down on me when it fell.

Yet, as I think about it now, I realize how much I got from the experience. I have many friends I wouldn't have known without it. I learned how to do sales well—although it's something I usually prefer to avoid. I learned so much about the region around the Finger Lakes. I began doing travel and event reviews. My photography improved. If I thought very long, I could probably list at least 15 benefits I received as a result of taking that risk, even though it failed.

In the greater scheme of failures, it was pretty minor, except the damage to our family's finances. No one was killed or hurt. No one lost millions of dollars. No one's reputation was smeared. And I and my family are probably the only ones who thought about it for any time at all after it happened. I had to keep reminding myself of those facts.

I'm pleased to share that, once I got over it, I have gone on to undertake some of the projects of which I am most proud.

There are enormous risks taken and failures experienced every day by movie and Broadway producers, athletes, politicians, scientists, and companies like Apple, Disney and Toyota. The difference is, their mistakes are usually much higher stakes and very visible. In those cases, failures can cost enormous money and others' jobs.

The thing anyone who invests in risk to make their living must embrace is that, when you fall, you must rise up again to grasp success. They also know that, if you never try, you'll never make an error. But you can also never succeed either. You only truly fail when you give up.

I like what Winston Churchill had to say about failure: "Success is not final; failure is not fatal: it is the courage to continue that counts."

So go forth and flop…proudly. Then learn from your mistakes and boldly move on to your next victory!

It's In the Cards
2024

Have you ever thought about what you wanted to be, as a kid? How many of your dreams came true?

Most people I know have veered from the paths they originally envisioned, often with great satisfaction.

My first career goal was to be a volcanologist. I can hear those who know me laughing at the thought of me traipsing around the rim of a volcano. Starting in fifth grade, I took every book the school had on volcanos out of the library. When that passion passed, I turned to zoology. That was short-lived. I always expected to be a journalist and/or writer, and I've managed to capture that dream and make it my own, albeit, not as originally anticipated.

In recent years, as I've perused employment ads, I've often noticed interesting listings and, in reviewing their sought-after skills or experience thought, "Well, it's too late for *that* door."

As I think about opportunity, I see life as a long corridor with many doors. The further down the hall you move, the fewer doors there are, and some are harder to open. Either you don't have, have never had the key, or you'd have had to stop and open it much sooner. But it's important to remember that the rooms behind those doors might not always have been as attractive as you imagined.

I can think of at least a half-dozen examples where I tried to go through certain doors to employment opportunities, and I didn't get the job. At the time, I was usually devastated. But in almost every case, within six to eighteen months, I learned some piece of information—that the company was going under, that the Board was a nightmare, that a new, maniacal CEO was hired—causing me to think, "Thank heavens it wasn't in the cards for me to get *that* job."

The thing is, just because some doors are closed doesn't mean there aren't exciting other "doors" down the hallway, including some that you may not see from where you're standing. Inevitably, new opportunities come along when you actively seek them out and you're ready to go through them by having acquired new skills and information.

Whether you're looking go through a door to a different full- or part-time job, to acquire additional clients, or to participate in an exciting hobby you've never tried before, that opportunity will be in the cards and the door will open, if you play your hand right.

No Imposter
2024

Years ago, when I was single and living in Bay Ridge, Brooklyn, my roommate Diane and I would occasionally go to an Irish bar on Saturday night. The music was good, the drinks were reasonably priced, and a fun group of locals hung out there.

One night, when she and I were talking to two different groups of people, Diane came over to me and whispered, "See that guy over there in the blue shirt? He asked about you and I told him you're with the CIA. Play along with me."

Very soon, he materialized at my side and said, "So, your friend tells me you're with the CIA."

"Did she? How odd."

He then began to dig for information. In the mode of "playing along," but not willing to lie either, I neither confirmed nor denied his suspicions. I simply responded to his inquiries with answers that were honest about the *true* me, but not about the *me* he *thought I was*.

"So, do you travel a lot for work?" He asked.

"A fair amount." (I was a meetings professional at a trade association at that point, and we held events across the country).

"Do you go overseas a lot?"

"Occasionally." (Also true. We held events in conjunction with our European trade association counterpart about every two years).

Oddly, the less information I gave him, the more mysterious I became, apparently convincing him of my secret identity. While I gave truths about my real job, he assumed I was referring to the role he *imagined* I held.

At one point, I actually said, "If I were with the CIA or FBI, do you *really* think I'd tell a roommate that?"

I could tell by the look on his face that this comment had clinched my identity for him and nothing I could have said after that would have dissuaded him of his conviction. If I were to even try to deny it, the more firmly entrenched his belief would become.

Eventually my roommate and I left to go find a quieter place to grab a bite to eat, but I'm sure tales of my identity trailed me out the door like ghosts.

Why do I mention this? It is important because of what we know as the Imposter Syndrome, where high-achieving people doubt their intellect, skills, or accomplishments.

In a writing group I just joined, some of the members in the group who are writing, and even those who have had work published, talked about the fact that they often don't feel like "real" writers. They mentioned varying reasons…

they don't write often enough...their work hasn't been picked up by an agent or they haven't been published by "a serious press"... they don't make their living as a full-time writer (who does?!)....

If *complete strangers* can believe we are someone we *are not*, why do we have such a hard time believing we are the competent, complete person we *are*? Why do we find dozens of ways and reasons to minimize ourselves and our accomplishments?

Perhaps we would do well to step outside ourselves and ask the kind of questions a stranger might ask us. In that way, we might be able to see ourselves more clearly and recognize that we've allowed ourselves to be minimized by a a quirky psychological phenomenon when, in fact, we possess *authentic* skills and talents, and in fact, there are *no imposters* in the room.

All That You Are
2023

"To shine your brightest light is to be who you truly are."

– Roy T. Bennett

How often do you stop and think about all that you are?

I think it's a pretty common human trait to think about all the things that we *aren't*. We berate ourselves because we're not better at math or finance, we chide ourselves because we're not as committed as we want to be at losing weight, we go directly to self-criticism because we're not better at a sport, at cooking, at art, or at finance. Stop and ask how important what you're beating yourself up over really is.

When we focus on what we *lack,* we overlook all that we are: all the skills and experience we've acquired, how much we mean to our friends and family, what we contribute at work and in the community. That "I am not" focus is a glass half-empty perspective to which many of us fall victim, myself included.

So how do we control that impulse? Below is a list of seven ideas to help remind us of all that we are.

1. Write down all you've achieved in your life. Be generous and include all the things of which you are most proud, including both the "small," as well as the most significant accomplishments. Remember: A large and beautiful garden is composed of many lovely, individual flowers of *all* sizes.

2. List all the people who love and care about you. Include both those from your past and your present.

3. Practice an "attitude of gratitude," and make a regular discipline of "the grateful heart," focusing on both your attributes as well as the many people, activities, and things that enrich your life.

4. Ask friends or family to share what their favorite aspects are of your personality. I bet you'll find some rewarding surprises.

5. Find colleagues or people among your network to connect with as a support system when you are lacking confidence and feeling "less than yourself," and need a boost.

6. If there's a skill you'd like to attain, you can achieve it, and it doesn't have to break the bank to do so! There's never been a better time to learn new things with the many free or low price online classes, the library, and community groups that offer specialized training.

7. List all of the obstacles you've overcome in your life, and in a second column, list the things you have learned as a result, and the strength you have gained through them.

I invite all of us to embrace, celebrate, and share all that we are! There is rich reward and power in embracing that knowledge and confidence.

Acknowledgements

I have many to thank for inspiring this book, especially my friends and family members who wander through these pages, providing both inspiration and humorous anecdotes. Know that I love and appreciate you all! If you find yourself the subject of this humor, please trust that I am a believer in what my mother used to say: "You don't tease people you don't love or care about."

If you haven't *yet* appeared in this book, don't take it personally. Let me assure you that, although you may not *seem* to have been a source of inspiration or the target for the slings and arrows of outrageous humor *in this book*, it doesn't mean you haven't inspired or amused me, or that I don't care about you. The operative word is *yet*! I am not giving up writing anytime soon.

I include a special note of thanks to my husband Ted and our daughters Danielle and Nicole. You inspire me and make me laugh every day.

My gratitude also goes out to my dear friend Debra Ross of KidsOutAndAbout.com who invited me to become Editor of BeyondtheNest.com back in 2017. The discipline of writing a weekly post for more than seven years has made me a better, more passionate writer. I also thank her for giving permission to include some of my favorite BeyondtheNest columns in this book.

I also owe a debt of thanks to my close friends Liz Nally and Kathy Porter who reviewed this in advance of publication and provided input to ensure the pieces were universal. Many thanks as well to my dear friends Wendy Kout and Susan Amesse for their invaluable and heartfelt comments that truly touched me.

I thank Sister Diana Dolce for the opportunity to work with her on her upcoming book. That experience has been encouraging, uplifting, and has reminded me of how much I love book design and all things literature-related.

I also thank our BeyondtheNest readers, many of whom have responded to surveys, editorials and/or sent notes of encouragement and support over these years, which is always heartwarming for a writer, and very much appreciated.

If I have left anyone out (other than our cat LeeLee, whose paws traipsing across the keyboard have created some very peculiar spellings, and whose proofreading skills leave something to be desired), please know that you are included in my heart, if not in my words.

Lastly, many thanks to you, dear reader, for having chosen to "take a chance" on *Laughing with the gods*. I know there are many choices of how you spend your resources, especially your time, and I am grateful that you have elected to spend some of yours with me!

Until the next book, I am...

Lightheartedly yours,

Carol

Thank You for Reading
Laughing with the gods

If you enjoyed this book, I would be grateful
if you would leave a review on Amazon,
Goodreads, or the site
from which you purchased this book!

If you would like to send me a note or
join my mailing list, please visit:
www.CommuniVisionStudio.com

www.ingramcontent.com/pod-product-compliance
Lightning Source LLC
LaVergne TN
LVHW051113080426
835510LV00018B/2012